EMPIRES OF ANCIENT MESOPOTAMIA

GREAT EMPIRES OF THE PAST

EMPIRES OF ANCIENT MESOPOTAMIA

BARBARA A. SOMERVILL

LESLIE SCHRAMER, HISTORICAL CONSULTANT

CHELSEA HOUSE
PUBLISHERS

An imprint of Infobase Publishing

Great Empires of the Past: Empires of Ancient Mesopotamia

Copyright © 2010 Barbara A. Somervill

Chelsea House
An imprint of Infobase Publishing
132 West 31st Street
New York NY 10001

Library of Congress Cataloging-in-Publication Data

Somervill, Barbara A.
  Empires of ancient Mesopotamia / Barbara A. Somervill.
    p. cm. — (Great empires of the past)
  Includes bibliographical references and index.
  ISBN 978-1-60413-157-4 (acid-free paper) 1. Iraq—Civilization—To 634—Juvenile literature. I. Title. II. Series.

  DS69.5.S65 2009
  935—dc22
                              2009017740

Chelsea House books are available at special discounts when purchased in bulk quantities for businesses, associations, institutions, or sales promotions. Please call our Special Sales Department in New York at (212) 967-8800 or (800) 322-8755.

You can find Chelsea House on the World Wide Web at http://www.chelseahouse.com

Produced by the Shoreline Publishing Group LLC
Editorial Director: James Buckley Jr.
Series Editor: Beth Adelman
Text design by Annie O'Donnell
Cover design by Alicia Post
Composition by Mary Susan Ryan-Flynn
Cover printed by Bang Printing, Brainerd, MN
Book printed and bound by Bang Printing, Brainerd, MN
Date printed: December 2009

Printed in the United States of America

10 9 8 7 6 5 4 3 2 1

CONTENTS

INTRODUCTION

FEW CULTURES HAVE HAD AS BIG AN IMPACT ON MODERN society as the empires of ancient Mesopotamia. Their influence can be seen in almost every area, including mathematics, writing, agriculture, and architecture. It was Mesopotamian scholars who developed the idea of using zero as a number. They also developed writing and they founded the first schools.

In agriculture, early Mesopotamian farmers understood the importance of maintaining a surplus (extra) of food so they could eat even in bad years. They used seeds from wild plants to produce crops, and invented a plow that planted seeds as it turned over the soil. They also domesticated farm animals (bred them to be used specifically for agriculture). Since the climate was dry, they needed to bring water from elsewhere for their crops, so they developed an irrigation system (bringing water to crops through canals or ditches). The ability to create a steady food supply meant that the Mesopotamians could settle in one location and build a community

Mesopotamians were also the people who invented a process for making glass. They designed arches, columns, and domes for their buildings, as well. And, in perhaps the most basic invention of all, they developed the wheel for use in transportation.

THE GEOGRAPHY OF MESOPOTAMIA

Mesopotamia was not a single nation or a single culture. It was a large region that today spreads through Iraq and parts of Syria and Tur-

CONNECTIONS

What Are Connections?

Throughout this book, and all the books in the Great Empires of the Past series, there are Connections boxes. They point out ideas, inventions, art, food, customs, and more from this empire that are still part of the world today. Nations and cultures in remote history can seem far away from the present day, but these connections demonstrate how our everyday lives have been shaped by the peoples of the past.

key. The name *Mesopotamia* is Greek, and means "the land between the rivers." The rivers are the Tigris and the Euphrates. Mesopotamia covers all the land between these two rivers, which were crucial for the region's development.

The region is bounded to the north and east by the Zagros and Taurus mountain ranges. To the south lies the Arabian Plateau and the Persian Gulf, and to the west the Syrian Desert. The northern area is made up of rolling hills and sweeping plains. Seasonal rains wash the land and fill the rivers and streams.

When human beings first arrived in the area, they found forests, mountains, and fresh water. Far to the south lie marshes that are thick with reeds. The wetlands are broad and flat. There are no great forests or hills. Over thousands of years, the climate has changed very little. Winters are cold and wet. Summers are long, hot, and very dry.

In Mesopotamia, the rivers, more than any other land feature, allowed civilization to grow and thrive. Each spring, snow melted in the northern mountains, sending water rushing along the rivers. The water carried fertile soil, which it deposited on the fields when the rivers overflowed. These deposits allowed for high-yield farming in an area that would otherwise have been too harsh to grow crops. The rivers also provided fresh water for drinking and washing, fish to eat, and transportation for travelers and traders.

The ancient Mesopotamian cultures saw a need to control the rivers' flow. They built protective dikes (low walls, usually made of earth, built to keep out water) to prevent cities from being flooded. They dug canals to channel the water and to irrigate their crops. They built docks from which to launch the reed sailboats they made to travel along the rivers.

Today, dams, dikes, and canals still control the flow of the Tigris and the Euphrates Rivers. The rivers also still provide fresh water, fish, and transportation for the peoples of the region.

UNCOVERING MESOPOTAMIA

The earliest people of Mesopotamia were hunter-gatherers. These people lived in clans (groups of close-knit families) and did not have permanent homes. They hunted game animals and gathered wild fruit, roots, nuts, and berries to feed themselves. When the clans had killed all the game in one area, they moved on to find a new hunting site. Those roaming clans eventually became farmers and, over time, built towns and cities. This change took several thousand years.

The people living in different cities spoke different languages and had different religious beliefs. Their customs and lifestyles were different as well. The only thing they shared was the land on which they lived. The desire to possess the land set one group against another in what seems like endless years of war.

Over thousands of years, many cultures rose and fell in Mesopotamia. Among the most powerful were the Sumerians, the Babylonians, and the Assyrians. These cultures left a remarkably clear history behind. People today can read about them in the Old Testament of the Bible. People can also study their cultures in the ruins of ancient cities. Most of these cities lay buried beneath tons of rubble for more than 2,000 years. Uncovering these cities in the 1800s and 1900s created rivalries between scientists.

Archaeology (the study of ancient people and cultures) in its early stages was like a match between sports teams. In the mid-1800s, the British and the French led the field. They argued over who got to dig where and tried to sabotage each other. As they dug up tombs, burial grounds, and entire cities, the two nations sent home the wealth of the Middle East to fill their museums and private collections with artifacts (items made by humans, such as pottery or tools). It never occurred to them that the precious items they dug up might not belong to them.

The two archaeologists who dominated the digs in Mesopotamia were Austen Henry Layard (1817–1894) of Britain and Paul Emile Botta (1802–1870) of France. Botta and Layard sought to uncover at

The Fertile Crescent

Mesopotamia has been called the Fertile Crescent and the cradle of civilization. The name *Fertile Crescent* comes from the shape of the land, which is similar to a crescent moon. Desert surrounds the crescent, but within that region fruit, vegetables, and grain grow quickly. *The cradle of civilization* refers to a number of different places where people built new cultures, founded cities and governments, and established agriculture. The area of the Fertile Crescent is often considered the cradle of civilization because it was also the place where writing began. China, India, and Egypt have also been thought of as cradles of civilization.

Uncovering a Great Treasure

In 1854, British archaeologist Austen Henry Layard published a book called *A Popular Account of Discoveries at Nineveh*, in which he described his activities in Mesopotamia and what he found. At one point, he thought he would never find anything worthwhile in the ruins. Then, his men made a remarkable find. In this section, he describes how the Black Obelisk of Shalmaneser III, one of Assyria's greatest treasures, was uncovered.

An *obelisk* is a four-sided stone column that tapers to a point on top. *Inscriptions* are words that are carved into a hard surface. A *vizier* is a type of ancient governor and *eunuchs* are a special kind of servants. *Tribute* is a tax paid to a ruler, usually by those conquered in war, and in this case, *tributaries* are people who pay tribute.

These are the wooden gates from the palace of Assyrian king Shalmaneser III. The bottom detail shows the Assyrians attacking a city. The top part shows porters and Assyrian officers.

I mounted my horse; but had scarcely left the mound when the corner of a monument in black marble was uncovered, which proved to be an obelisk, about six feet six inches in height, lying on its side, ten feet below the surface.

An Arab was sent after me without delay, to announce the discovery; and on my return I found, completely exposed to view, an obelisk terminated by three steps . . . and flat at the top. I descended eagerly into the trench, and was immediately struck by the singular appearance, and evident antiquity, of the remarkable monument before me. We raised it and speedily dragged it out of the ruins. On each side were five small bas-reliefs, and above, below, and

between them was carved an inscription 210 lines in length. The whole was in the best preservation. The king was twice represented followed by his attendants; a prisoner was at his feet, and his vizier and eunuchs were introducing captives and tributaries carrying vases, shawls, bundles of rare wood, elephant's tusks, and other objects of tribute, and leading various animals, among which were the elephant, the rhinoceros, the Bactrian or two-humped camel, the wild bull, and several kinds of monkeys. In one bas-relief were two lions hunting a stag in a wood, probably to denote the nature of one of the countries conquered by the king.

(Source: Layard, Austen Henry. *A Popular Account of Discoveries at Nineveh*. Available online. http://www.aina.org/books/dan. htm#chapter9. Accessed March 21, 2008.)

least part of the famed fabulous wealth of ancient Assyria. They were digging in an area near Mosul (in today's Iraq).

As the story goes, Botta was a bored French government official living in Mosul. One day he was shopping in the local suq (the Arabic word for an open-air marketplace) and was looking through the piles of fake and real artifacts offered for sale. He bargained for a better price in fluent Arabic, and this caught the attention of local traders. The traders told Botta that they knew a place where the types of pots and statuettes they were selling lay everywhere. Lead by these traders, Botta began exploring the massive mounds around the northern Tigris River. These earth mounds were thought to cover valuable ruins of ancient Assyrian cities. Botta's most spectacular finds included sculptures, bas-relief wall panels (carved sculpture

This is a sickle, a tool used for cutting grain. As farmers learned more efficient farming techniques, they were able to produce more food than they needed for themselves and their families.

in which the figures stand out from the background), and decorated bricks from the palace at Dur-Sharrukin (an ancient Assyrian capital, modern Khorsabad).

Around the same time, Layard began digging in the same area. Botta had decided that Mosul was French territory, and he was not pleased. Neither archaeologist recognized that the local government owned the ruins that lay beneath the earth. Layard was living at a dig site at Nineveh when he heard that the local pasha (governor) said all digging was to stop. Layard hurried to Mosul to see the pasha, who claimed to have no problems with Layard's digging. Layard returned to the digs, only to be called back to the pasha's palace.

This time, the pasha claimed that he was worried about Layard's welfare. Threats had been made against Layard because he had been digging in a sacred (holy) area—a cemetery. Layard was confused. In weeks of digging he had not seen any tombstones, bodies, bones, or any other sign of a graveyard. For two days, Layard and the pasha argued. Finally, Layard was allowed to return to his dig—only to find a complete cemetery in place where none had been before!

The truth came out: The pasha had ordered his men to move a cemetery onto Layard's site to stop the British from further digging. Who was behind this trickery? It was Botta, who wanted the riches of Layard's dig for France.

Layard finally got permission to continue digging. From 1845 to 1848, Layard dug at Nimrud, an ancient Assyrian city located south of Nineveh on the Tigris River in today's Iraq.

Layard later uncovered the great library of Ashurbanipal, which contained 24,000 clay slabs, called *tablets*, with

CONNECTIONS

Wheels Drive Progress

Everyone who rides a bicycle or drives a car should thank the Sumerians. More than 5,000 years ago, a brilliant Sumerian craftsman decided that hauling heavy goods would be much easier if they were rolled rather than dragged along the ground. That idea led to the development of vehicles with wheels.

The first Sumerian wheels were made of solid slabs of wood, held on an axle (the rod that connects two wheels) with wooden or metal brackets. Wheels with spokes, like the ones on a bike, did not appear until about 2000 B.C.E. Wheels made it easy to carry goods in a wagon, particularly when that wagon was attached to another Mesopotamian development—domesticated oxen and donkeys.

writing on them. He also found more than 70 rooms, many decorated with bas-reliefs and murals (pictures made right on the wall) retelling the triumphs of the great Assyrian king Shalmaneser III (r. 858–824 B.C.E.), along with hundreds of other artifacts. Many of Layard's discoveries are on display in the British Museum in London.

Since the days when Botta and Layard fought over who could collect Mesopotamia's great treasures, dozens of archaeologists have dug into

CONNECTIONS

Hard Envelopes, No Licking

When kings, officials, and traders of Mesopotamia needed to send private information, they did what is still done today: They put their messages in envelopes. These envelopes were not made of paper, but of clay. A scribe (a person who makes a living by writing down official records) wrote the letter on a clay tablet. The tablet was allowed to harden. Then the tablet was enclosed in an outer layer of clay and marked with the receiver's address and the sender's seal. When the letter arrived, the receiver cracked the outer envelope, removed the tablet, and read the document.

the region's history. They have uncovered thousands of documents, including letters still in their hard clay envelopes. They have found bas-reliefs and mosaics (pictures or decorations made from small pieces of colored tile) that tell the story of kings long dead and empires now fallen to ruin.

Digging continues to this day, and the finds reveal much about these lost cultures. At one dig in 1989, archaeologists and their crews swept away rubble to reveal some remarkable technology in an ancient burial tomb. They found ceramic pipes that had been part of an air vent. There was a stone door that swung smoothly on carved stone hinges. There was also a stone coffin, called a sarcophagus, with an eerie warning: "If anyone lays hands on my tomb, let the ghost of insomnia take hold of him for ever and ever" (quoted in Philp Elmer-Dewitt's *Time* magazine story, "The Golden Treasures of Nimrud"). If the archaeologists lost any sleep over disturbing the tomb, it was probably due to the thrill of the other things they found in the burial place: pounds of delicate golden trinkets and cylinder seals dating back nearly 2,500 years. (Cylinder seals were small, carved tubes that owners rolled in wet clay. Each seal was unique to its owner and represented the owner's signature.) Another nearby tomb held 440 artifacts, including golden jewelry, statues, and vases.

More Than Ordinary Interest

In his 1854 book, *A Popular Account of Discoveries at Nineveh*, British archaeologist Austen Henry Layard tried to explain what drove him to dig through the ancient cities of Mesopotamia.

"The ruins in Assyria and Babylonia, chiefly huge mounds, apparently of mere earth and rubbish, had long excited curiosity from their size and evident antiquity. They were the only remains of an unknown period. They alone could be identified with Nineveh and Babylon, and could afford a [clue] to the . . . nature of those cities. There is, at the same time, a vague mystery attached to remains like these, which induces travelers to examining them with more than ordinary interest."

The wealth and beauty of these finds continues to surprise archaeologists and historians. How did these ancient people make such exquisite artwork? Do the bas-relief scenes of wars provide accurate historical accounts of events? How can historians create a complete picture of the ancient civilizations using the boasts of a conquering king, the list of goods sold by a merchant, and the curse of a body whose bones have turned to dust? Only further study of Mesopotamia can answer these questions.

PART · 1

HISTORY

FROM FARM TO CITY

FROM SARGON TO HAMMURABI

THE FINAL YEARS OF POWER

CHAPTER 1

FROM FARM TO CITY

ABOUT 12,000 YEARS AGO, HUMAN BEINGS BEGAN MOVING into the land between the two rivers that are now known as the Tigris River and the Euphrates River. At first, these people were hunter-gatherers. As the populations of these people grew, and as they developed better tools, it eventually became more practical for them to stop wandering from place to place, following the animals they hunted.

By 9000 B.C.E., clans began developing small settlements. They no longer went out searching for their food, and increasingly started to rely on food they produced. This is when farming began. It took several months to plant, grow, and harvest a crop, so it was logical for families to build stronger, more permanent settlements.

The people in the region now called Mesopotamia built small villages with round huts. Most houses were cut into the ground, and people used a ladder to enter. The average hut had a roof of twigs, reeds, and leaves. Inside, there was a stone hearth (fireplace) in the center and areas around the hearth for sitting or sleeping.

The first plows were probably just sticks used to dig holes. But Mesopotamia's early farmers soon developed better plows—and a better way to pull those plows. They tamed wild animals to pull plows and provide milk and meat. Over the same time period, farmers discovered that they could grow grain, dry it, and grind it into flour. This meant that food crops harvested in the fall could be eaten through the winter.

Two early cultures emerged in Mesopotamia in about 7500 B.C.E. These were the Hassuna and the Samarra peoples. These people developed pottery, used stone tools, and spun thread from flax and wool. They carved stones to make beads and pendants for jewelry. Copper

OPPOSITE
The Standard of Ur is a hollow wooden box found in the remains of the ancient Sumerian city-state of Ur. This part shows soldiers in the middle and war chariots on the top and bottom. Archaeologists are not sure what the box was used for.

CONNECTIONS

Domestication of Animals

Domesticated animals are animals that have been tamed to be used in agriculture or to live and work with people. These animals include pets and livestock. Here is a list of animals from the Middle East and the approximate time they became domesticated.

Animal	Wild Relative	Approximate Year of Domestication (B.C.E.)
Dog	Wolf	11,000
Goat	Bezoar goat	8500
Sheep	Moufflon	8000
Pig	Boar	7500
Cow	Auroch	7000
Cat	North African wildcat	7000
Donkey	Wild ass	4000

was commonly used for tools and jewelry. The Samarra produced beautiful pottery decorated with brown designs. The Hassuna and Samarra peoples advanced agriculture, growing several varieties of wheat and barley, as well as flax (a plant whose fiber is used to make cloth).

By 6000 B.C.E., northern Mesopotamia was well settled. The Hassuna and Samarra cultures gave way to a new group, called the Halaf. The Halaf people thrived for nearly 600 years and spread throughout northern Mesopotamia. The land where the Halaf lived was ideal for farming, with rich, fertile soil, plenty of rainfall, and rivers and streams for fresh water. It was also home to native plants and animals that were suited to being domesticated. In addition to wheat and barley, the people grew lentils, bitter vetch (a kind of pea), and chickpeas.

THE RISE OF CITIES

In the south, the Ubaidian culture emerged. The Ubaid lived in small farming groups that slowly evolved into towns. The farmers produced more grain and vegetables than they needed. They traded extra products with people who had stone, wood, metal, and other goods that were not found in farming communities. Trade along the Tigris and the Euphrates Rivers expanded, and, by 4000 B.C.E., towns exploded into cities. The first such cities included Eridu and Uruk.

The rise of cities brought a change in how society was organized. Groups of people banded together. They spoke a common language and, as a group, they claimed the right to control specific pieces of land. Leaders arose within the group and social classes were formed. The

This clay bull is in the style of the Ubaid culture.

wealthy class included rulers or nobles, priests, and scholars (people dedicated to learning and study). The middle class included mostly merchants, craftsmen, and, in some cases, the military. Peasants and slaves made up the lower classes.

Religion played a central role in city life. Every city had its own temples and its favorite gods. In larger cities, the favored or patron god (a god who was the special protector of a region or a group of people) may have changed from one neighborhood to the next. Early Mesopotamians believed in hundreds of spirits, gods, and goddesses. Different occupations—such as scribe, merchant, or builder—also had their own patron god who looked out for their welfare.

There were a few gods that most people followed. They were responsible for the major areas of the Mesopotamian universe—the sky, the earth, and the underworld. An was the father of all gods. He lived in and ruled over the sky. Enlil was the god of the air, while Utu reigned as the god of the sun, truth, and justice. Nanna was the god of the moon. Love and war came under the guidance of the goddess

Inanna, while Ninhursag was goddess of wild animals. Enki was the god of water, wisdom, and magic.

People needed a place to worship their gods and offer sacrifices. So temples were built to honor the gods. As cities grew, so did the size of the temples, their functions, and their wealth.

THE SUMERIANS

In about 3500 B.C.E., the Sumerians emerged as a distinct culture along the banks of the Euphrates River. The land they occupied needed to be drained to make it useful, and the Sumerians were able to solve this problem. They dug canals, which rerouted the water and divided the marshes into farmland and water. They built large cities that held a thriving culture and became the foundation of an advanced civilization.

Many historians have related the rise of Sumer with the discovery of bronze. In about 3100 B.C.E., Sumerian metalworkers found that combining copper and tin produced an outstandingly useful metal: bronze. Bronze was stronger and longer lasting than either copper or tin. It was the ideal metal for making tools, weapons, and statues. The Bronze Age began, and brought with it changes in the tools and weapons used by people of the region. The use of bronze would later spread throughout Europe and Asia.

The Sumerians were different from other cultures of the time. They organized their civilization to address the needs of their people. Engineering canals to create farmland required a large labor force. The efforts of these workers made it possible to produce enough food to support a large population. Farmers used more effective plows that

The First City

Today, the site of Eridu lies in the desert. But 8,000 years ago, it sat on the banks of the Euphrates River. Eridu was a religious center dedicated to the god of water, called Enki. According to legend, it was the first city ever established. The rise of Eridu as a city is retold in an ancient Babylonian epic poem (a long poem about history or heroes from the past). Here is a small portion of that epic poem (quoted in Michael Roaf's *Cultural Atlas of Mesopotamia and the Ancient Near East*).

> A reed had not come forth,
> A tree had not been created,
> A house had not been made,
> A city had not been made,
> All the lands were sea,
> Then Eridu was made.

When Did Writing Begin?

When archaeologists began digging through the ancient ruins of Mesopotamia, they found many clay tablets covered with triangular marks. They named the marks cuneiform, from the Latin word *cuneus*, meaning "wedge." The marks clearly meant something, but figuring out what they meant was not easy. Archaeologists compared symbols from one document to another, putting together the pieces of the puzzle.

Researchers cracked the code of cuneiform in the 1850s. These early archaeologists believed that writing in Mesopotamia began with pictographs (pictures used to represent words in a writing system) and advanced from there to cuneiform.

In the 1970s, archaeologist Denise Schmandt-Besserat (b. 1933) disagreed with these earlier theories. Schmandt-Besserat, former professor of art and Middle Eastern studies at the University of Texas, Austin, believed that writing first began in about 3200 B.C.E. during the Sumerian Empire. She claimed that Sumerian officials needed to record the crops, livestock, and oil produced by farmers to determine how much they should pay in taxes. They made those records by pressing symbols into wet clay. Those early farm records eventually evolved into the form of writing known as cuneiform, used by the Sumerians, Babylonians, and Assyrians.

Said Schmandt-Besserat, "It all began about 7500 B.C.E., when early farmers became concerned with keeping track of goods. They made counters out of clay in a dozen shapes, including cones, spheres, disks, cylinders, tetrahedrons [pyramids with three sides], and ovoids [oval shapes]. Each shape was assigned a meaning. A cone . . . stood for a small measure of grain; a cylinder stood for an animal. . . . It was the first visual code, the first symbol system ever created for the sole purpose of communicating." (quoted in the January/February 2002 issue of *Odyssey*) Four thousand years later, the tokens and counters gave way to an accounting system with several hundred shapes. This was the beginning of writing.

were pulled by oxen. This enabled the Sumerians to expand farming from tiny plots to large fields. The canals and irrigation guaranteed a successful crop that was not affected by drought (long periods without rain).

The Sumerians also developed wheeled chariots (two-wheeled carts) and carts pulled by donkeys. These carts enabled them to move

The handle on this cylinder seal is in the form of a sheep. The image on the right was made when the seal was rolled out. It shows a shepherd feeding his sheep. This seal is made of marble and copper.

large quantities of goods to markets beyond their own cities. The Sumerians had access to water, and when they developed ships with sails, they could sell their goods even farther from home. And so, the Sumerians advanced from farming for individual families to farming for entire cities. Then, the crops harvested became the basis of trade with other cultures.

Of greater importance was the Sumerian ability to communicate. The development of cuneiform script enabled people to record output, write letters, send news to others, and enter into business contracts. The Sumerians did not use paper for their documents. They used what they had the most of—mud. They filled a tray with wet clay, smoothed the surface, and wrote their documents. When the mud dried, they had a record of the information on a hard clay tablet. Many of those records exist today.

SUMERIAN CITY-STATES

Sumer was not a single country. It was a region made up of city-states (a city-state is a city and its surrounding farms that functions as a separate nation). Each city-state had its own ruler and noble class. Each had its own independent economy. There was no central capital, government, or ruler until about 2800 B.C.E. The major Sumerian city-states included Eridu, Nippur, Lagash, Uruk, Kish, and Ur. All were built beside either the Tigris or the Euphrates Rivers. High earthen dikes protected the cities from flooding and controlled the water used for irrigating crops.

Large plots of farmland surrounded the cities, and that land was considered the property of the local gods. Each individual temple owned lands that were considered the estate of the god the temple was dedicated to.

Each person in a city-state belonged to one of the temples, and the whole of a temple community—the officials and priests, herdsmen and fishermen, gardeners, craftsmen, stonecutters, merchants, and even slaves—was referred to as the people of the god of that temple.

Groups of workers farmed the land, following the directions of a priest. Priests were highly respected in the Sumerian community and were more than just religious leaders. They were sometimes also scientists, scholars, and community managers. Priests might also be scribes and teachers.

The work of every member of the community was valued, and all shared in the wealth of their community. For example, farming was a community effort and all members of the community shared in the harvest. Crops included barley and wheat for flour, beans, olives, and grapes. The community also raised cattle, sheep, and goats. A fisherman's catch was shared among the others, and the fisherman's family received a portion of barley, wheat, and grapes from the community harvest.

Temple lands were divided into three sections. Most of the land was farmed as a community. However, some farmland was rented for personal use. The rental fee was a share of the crop's value, paid at harvest time. Temple priests and officials could also use small sections of land for themselves. They paid no land use fees. Land use was one of the privileges of holding a temple office.

The people lived in small houses that were built like one-story apartments. Each home had a separate entrance but shared inside walls with other homes. Many houses opened onto community courtyards or gardens. Craftsmen, farmers, merchants, and their families lived within the protection of the city walls.

While farmers were responsible for producing the food eaten by the community, craftsmen turned out both practical and luxury products. Jewelers made finely wrought necklaces, bracelets, and rings. Carpenters built homes, furniture, and storage units. Weavers turned wool and flax into cloth, which was sewn into clothing. Tanners made leather goods, and blacksmiths produced metal tools.

How Do Cities Move?

Today, the sites of many of the early Sumerian city-states are no longer located beside rivers. It is not the cities that moved away from the river, but the river that moved from the cities. Flooding, damming, and time all make a river slowly change its course. This is called *meandering*.

Although leaders changed, the center of Sumerian life did not. The importance of one's city-state was central. In the same way that people today might say they are from Great Britain or Japan, Sumerians claimed their city-state as their home. "I am from Uruk," they might say.

People lived in Uruk for 5,000 years, from the early days of the Ubaid culture beyond the time of Mesopotamia's greatest empires. Uruk was a walled city that is currently known as Warka in Iraq. The city consisted of one-third temples, one-third homes, and one-third gardens. Within the city lay two major temples—the temple of An (god of the sky) and Eanna (House of Heaven), the temple of the goddess Inanna (goddess of love). In this temple's ruins, archaeologists found the oldest examples of writing.

Vegetables, grain, cloth, leather goods, jewelry, and hundreds of other items were sold in the open marketplace. Some people sold their own goods from stalls or off tables. Others sold their goods to merchants who put them on display. The Sumerian markets also had a variety of imported goods, brought from as far away as the coast of the Mediterranean Sea, the mountains in a region that is now Afghanistan, and the cities around the Persian Gulf.

A king ran the government of the city-state. The people believed this king was chosen by the gods to rule. Along with their kings, city-states had priests and a noble class. Most nobles were related to the king. The king protected his people from attack by raising an army that was paid for by tax money. He was also in charge of religious events, building city walls and irrigation canals, and keeping the peace among his subjects.

It was not possible for one person to do so many jobs, so the king had priests to run the temples, officers to lead the army, and officials to run the city. He also had scribes to record contracts, taxes, and other city business. Officials carefully monitored the sales of goods. Grain and other such items were weighed on scales, and the weights were accurate from one vendor to the next. This was another contribution the Mesopotamians made to the world—a standard of weights by which items were sold.

Merchants bought and sold goods to people who lived in the city or were visiting the city. They also carried extra products to other cities to trade. Reed boats with carefully woven sails enabled merchants to travel from city to city along the great rivers. The boats were made of the reeds that grew naturally in the area. (People living in the marshlands of southern Iraq use a similar type of reed boat today.) Land transportation depended on two other Mesopotamian developments—the wheel and domesticated animals. Donkeys and oxen pulled wheeled carts loaded with pottery, jewelry, and grains.

THE SUMERIAN KINGS

The easiest way to understand Sumer is to think of it as separate states in a region, each with its own king. At different times, one king became more powerful than the others. The first king to rule over the other Sumerian states was a king of Kish. Then a series of kings from Uruk rose to power.

The text on this tablet tells the legend of the first Sumerian king, Etana. It is written using cuneiform.

Much of what is known today about the Sumerian kings comes from legends and epic poems. Many of these legends were not written down until long after the kings died. Many of the deeds of these kings became exaggerated as the stories of their lives were passed down over generations. According to legend, some of these kings ruled for more than 1,000 years. One early record of the Sumerian kings is called the Kings List. If the list is to be believed, the first king, Etana, ruled for 1,560 years. Another king, Lugalbanda, supposedly was king for 1,200 years.

The first Sumerian king whose deeds were recorded for history was Etana (r. ca. 2800 B.C.E.), the king of Kish. Although Etana began as the king of one city-state, his power spread to include others. The information about Etana is vague. He was known as "he who stabilized all the

Rulers and Their Titles

Rulers of Sumerian city-states were given one of three different titles: *en* (lord), *ensi* (governor), or *lugal* (king). Each title carried with it specific responsibilities. Enmerkar, or Lord Merkar, had duties related to religion, and may have been a priest. Lugalbanda, or King Banda, had a title that had more to do with running a government than with religion. An *ensi* was a lower-ranking government official, much like a governor who reported to the *lugal*. When a king ruled over several city-states, he appointed *ensis* who took care of the day-to-day business of running smaller cities.

Is It a Date?

The people of Mesopotamia recorded events according to what they knew. For example, a battle took place in the fourth year of the reign of the current king. A new king came to power after the old king died and a new era began. So when Tiglathpileser I began his rule, that year became known as the first year of Tiglathpileser.

Historians have tried to fix dates to when specific kings ruled, but all dates are estimates. Two different historians may have figured out the dates based on information from different tablets and historical documents. As a result, the dates in which kings are said to have reigned may vary. Tiglathpileser I may have ruled from 1114 B.C.E. to 1076 B.C.E., or 1115 B.C.E. to 1077 B.C.E., or some other dates.

The letters *ca.* in front of a date mean *circa,* or *approximately*. It is not known when Mesopotamian kings were born, and those facts were not usually recorded. The dates that appear for Mesopotamian kings are about the time that each king ruled.

lands." What this title means is a guess, but historians think that when Etana ruled Kish, he may have had some power or influence in neighboring city-states. However, most historians agree that the Sumerian kings ruled only over their own city-states until the rise of Sargon I, the Akkadian king, in 2334 B.C.E.

Meskiaggasher (r. ca. 2775 B.C.E.) followed Etana, but he was not a king of Kish. Meskiaggasher founded a rival empire in Uruk, a city-state south of Kish. This empire was called the First Dynasty of Uruk. According to legend, Meskiaggasher was believed to be the son of Utu, the sun god. Meskiaggasher's son Enmerkar (r. ca. 2750 B.C.E.) was also called the son of Utu.

Enmerkar was a warrior king who battled to expand his empire. He was the priest-king of Uruk and is believed to be the first king to write on clay tablets. During the rule of Enmerkar, the first platform temples were built in Mesopotamia. The temples were early models of what would later be known as ziggurats (flat-topped, pyramid-shaped towers).

His reign was followed by that of a fellow warrior named Lugalbanda (r. ca. 2750–2700 B.C.E.), whose name means "small king." Lugalbanda appears in two epic poems, *Lugalbanda in the Mountain Cave* and *Lugalbanda and the Anzu Bird*. These legends describe Lugalbanda's military victories. In the legends, Lugalbanda is said to be the husband of the goddess Ninsun and father of Gilgamesh (r. ca. 2700 B.C.E.), a great king who was also the subject of an epic tale. The people of Sumer considered Lugalbanda to be a god.

Enmerkar and Lugalbanda became the heroes of many epic tales. These tales gave historians an insight into the history of the Sumerians. The legends explained to historians how Sumerian kings expanded their rule through battles with neighboring states. They told about politics and the power of the military. They also explained that kings were

The Epic of Gilgamesh

One of the many epic stories about the great kings of Sumer was about Gilgamesh. The most complete version of the text dates back to the seventh century C.E. This version was written on 12 tablets and found in the Akkadian city of Nineveh. The poem is actually much older, but this version provides the most text.

In Mesopotamia, the legend of Gilgamesh was told for centuries. The versions change slightly over time, but they are all the same basic story. The epic is the tale of a man named Gilgamesh and his close friend, Enkidu.

Gilgamesh was a king of Uruk and a hero to the Sumerian people—a wise king who was part god and part human. Gilgamesh and Enkidu set off on a series of adventures, including the search for immortality (the ability to live forever). On the way, they met gods and goddesses, performed feats of great strength and cleverness, experienced loss and sorrow, encountered floods, death, and demons, and received some sound advice on how to live a good life.

At one point in the legend, the goddess Inanna (known as Ishtar in some versions of the tale) tried to win Gilgamesh's love, but he rejected her. This showed great wisdom, because most of Inanna's lovers died tragically. Inanna tried to get revenge on Gilgamesh, but instead Enkidu died a horrible death. Gilgamesh mourns his friend deeply in this excerpt from the Gilgamesh epic.

Gilgamesh wept over Enkidu his friend,
Bitterly he wept through the wilderness.
"Must I die too? Must I be as lifeless
as Enkidu? How can I bear this sorrow
that gnaws at my belly, this fear of death
that restlessly drives me onward? If only
I could find the one man whom the gods
made immortal,
I would ask him how to overcome death."
So Gilgamesh roamed, his heart full of anguish,
Wandering, always eastward, in search
Of Utnapishtim, whom the god made immortal.

(Source: Mitchell, Stephen. *Gilgamesh: A New English Version.* New York: Free Press, 2006.

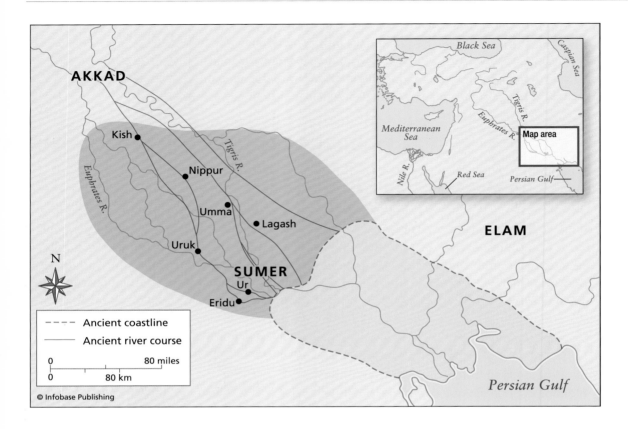

This map shows Sumer during the Early Dynastic Period, ca. 3000–2360 B.C.E. Sumer spread from the Persian Gulf, along the Tigris and Euphrates Rivers, to encompass the city-states of Kish, Uruk, and Ur. During this period, the coastline of the Persian Gulf extended several miles further inland than it does today.

believed to be gods and were treated like gods by their people. The two rulers were real people, but the tales about them seemed larger than life, much like the tales of Robin Hood or King Arthur. Lugalbanda's reign ended with his death, and his son Gilgamesh followed him.

Gilgamesh was also a legendary figure, although he was probably also a real person. He was born in Uruk some time around 2700 B.C.E. and became the fifth king of Sumer. Gilgamesh was, at times, a tyrant, a good friend, a boaster, and a hero. He ordered the building of walls around the city of Uruk.

In the legend, Gilgamesh had a series of adventures that angered the Sumerian gods. They punished him by taking the life of his best friend, Enkidu. Gilgamesh looked for, but could not find, a way to live forever. The Gilgamesh epic matches the Bible in many places. In the epic poem, a great flood pours over the Earth. This story is a lot like the Bible story of Noah and the flood.

About 50 years after the reign of Etana, another king of Kish dominated the region. This was Enmebaragesi (r. ca. 2750 B.C.E.), the king who conquered the state of Elam. Elam, an ancient civilization located in present-day Iran, existed from about 5000 B.C.E. to 539 B.C.E. As Sumer expanded, trade increased and the Sumerian people spread their language and religious beliefs. People also shared knowledge of agriculture, medicine, and science.

At some point, Enmebaragesi decided to build a large religious center in Nippur, which had been settled for centuries. The buildings included the temple of Enlil, the lord of the wind. Nippur grew into a sprawling religious center, which attracted travelers and traders. According to legend, Enmebaragesi reigned for 900 years. But, like many legends, this one stretched the truth—by about 850 years. Enmebaragesi's son Agga was defeated by Gilgamesh in about 2670 B.C.E.

About a hundred years later, another city rose to prominence. Mesanepada, the son a of king of Kish, became the new ruler of Sumer. He moved the empire's capital to Ur and founded the first dynasty of Ur. (A dynasty is a family that keeps control of a government over many generations, with rule often passed from a parent to a child.) Mesanepada's reign lasted about 80 years. Several lesser kings followed Mesanepada over the next several hundred years. Then, Sumer once again saw the rise of a great ruler, Lugalzagesi (r. ca. 2340–2316 B.C.E.). Lugalzagesi was an empire builder. He ruled as king of Uruk, Kish, Umma, Ur, and Lagash.

The change from one king to the next was not always easy. Sometimes a king followed his father, as was the case with Gilgamesh. At other times, rulers of smaller Sumerian city-states battled the ruling king for power. In ancient times, power equaled wealth. Kings collected taxes to built palaces, cities, and armies. When a king became too greedy, appeared weak, or died, another ruler rose up to take his place. The rise to becoming king often cost many lives. Eventually, the constant fighting over who would rule weakened Sumer. The empire could not both battle for power within Sumer and fend off attacks from outside. Lugalzagesi hired Semites from Akkad to serve in his army. However, these soldiers owed their loyalty to Sargon I (r. ca. 2334–2279 B.C.E.), the king of Akkad. With the rise of Sargon, the Sumerians' domination came to an end.

The Kings of Sumer

It is not possible to provide birth and death dates for the major kings of Sumer. Most dates represent an estimated time when historians believe a king reigned. The dynasties of Uruk and Kish were likely contemporary rather than sequential. As a result, some of the dates overlap.

Etana of Kish (ca. 2800 B.C.E.)

Meskiaggasher of Uruk (ca. 2775 B.C.E.)

Enmerkar of Uruk (ca. 2750 B.C.E.)

Lugalbanda of Uruk (ca. 2750–2700 B.C.E.)

Gilgamesh of Uruk (ca. 2700 B.C.E.)

Enmebaragesi of Kish (ca. 2750 B.C.E.)

Agga of Kish (ca. 2700 B.C.E.)

Mesanepada of Ur (ca. 2560–2525 B.C.E.)

Lugalzagesi of Uruk (ca. 2340–2316 B.C.E.)

CHAPTER 2

FROM SARGON TO HAMMURABI

THE POWER OF THE SUMERIAN KINGS ENDED IN 2334 B.C.E., when Sargon I (the Great) became king of Akkad and Sumer. Sargon ruled the kingdom of Akkad, and eventually expanded his empire over all Mesopotamia and into parts of modern Syria, Turkey, and western Iran.

Akkad lay to the northwest of Sumer. Unlike Sumer, which was made up of independent city-states, Akkad was a region whose cities were governed from a capital city, called Agade. Agade was a city on the Euphrates River between Sippar and Kish. Under Sargon, the influence of Akkad spread to encompass Sumer; thereafter, southern Mesopotamia was known as the land of Sumer and Akkad.

Almost everything modern historians know about Sargon comes from epic poems, legends, and tales written on clay tablets, stelae (stone pillars with inscriptions on them), and bas-reliefs. The legends relate that Sargon was the son of a high priestess (a woman who is the leader of a religious group) who gave birth to him in secret and abandoned him. The mother placed her infant son in a basket and set him adrift on the river. A gardener found the basket in a tangle of reeds and rescued the baby. The gardener raised the boy as his own son, and Sargon eventually became the cupbearer (a person responsible for providing the king's wine) of the king of Kish. This was an honored position, and it put Sargon in contact with many government officials.

As the legend continues, the king of Kish was killed by Lugalzagesi of Uruk. How this was done is not known. The legends relate that Sargon rallied the Kish army to defeat Lugalzagesi in 2334 B.C.E. and founded the Akkadian Empire.

OPPOSITE
This cast copper head probably represents Sargon the Great, who established the Akkadian Empire, or his grandson Naram-Sin.

IN THEIR OWN WORDS

A Plea to the Goddess Inanna

King Sargon's daughter, Enheduanna (ca. 2285–2250 B.C.E.), was both a poet and the high priestess of the goddess Inanna. She is the first known female poet in history. Enheduanna took her job as high priestess seriously and dedicated her life to serving Inanna, the goddess of love and fertility. When her father died, Enheduanna lost her job as high priestess. The new king, her brother Rimush, replaced her with another woman. In this poem, Enheduanna pleads with Inanna to recognize how badly she has been treated.

Me who once sat triumphant, he has driven out of the sanctuary.
Like a swallow he made me fly from the window,
My life is consumed.
He stripped me of the crown appropriate for the high priesthood. . . .

It was in your service that I first entered the holy temple,
I, Enheduanna, the highest priestess.
I carried the ritual basket,
I chanted your praise.
Now I have been cast out to the place of lepers.
Day comes and the brightness is hidden around me.
Shadows cover the light, drape it in sandstorms.
My beautiful mouth knows only confusion. . . .

(Source: "Ancient Tablets, Ancient Graves: Assessing Women's Lives in Mesopotamia." Women in World History. Available online. URL: http://www.womeninworldhistory.com/lesson2.html. Accessed March 17, 2008.)

Sargon was a brilliant military leader. Under his leadership, the Akkadians conquered all of Sumer and spread their influence to other lands. It is said that Sargon fought and won 34 battles across Mesopotamia and expanded his rule from present-day Iran in the east to Syria in the west, the Persian Gulf in the south, and into present-day Turkey in the north. He brought 50 *ensi* (governors) under his control. Sargon also expanded trade beyond Mesopotamia. He brought deep blue lapis lazuli (a semiprecious stone) from the mountains of Afghanistan and cedar wood from Lebanon to the lands of Sumer and Akkad.

Sargon was the first of several Akkadian rulers who made up the Akkadian dynasty. He was followed by Rimush, Manishtusu, Naram-Sin, and Shar-kali-sharri. Rimush, son of Sargon, ruled Akkad from about 2278 B.C.E. to 2270 B.C.E. He faced several rebellions against his rule, but he was able to suppress them all. When Rimush died, his brother Manishtusu (r. ca. 2269–2255 B.C.E.) took over. He was no more popular than Rimush and was killed by his own nobles.

The Akkadians ruled Mesopotamia for 141 years. At the height of their power, more than 65 cities fell under Akkadian rule. The Akkadians seemed always to be at war; they wanted to hold onto what they had and constantly add more territory. The Akkadian Empire covered a large area and transportation was slow, since it depended on donkey carts and riverboats. The slow transportation also limited communication between cities. The larger the empire grew, the harder it was to control the areas on the far borders.

THE AKKADIAN PEOPLE

The Akkadian people spoke a Semitic language. Semites were people from southwestern Asia, including Hebrews, Arabs, and Phoenicians. They spoke similar languages, but all were different from the language of Sumer. With the rise of the Akkadians, the people of Mesopotamia combined two cultures—Sumerian and Akkadian. They also combined two ways of communicating. They spoke Akkadian, and, over time, they learned to write Akkadian in cuneiform, the script developed by the Sumerians.

During the Akkadian period, craftsmen advanced their skills in architecture and sculpture. Elegant Akkadian palaces stood as powerful fortresses and featured large halls, bathing chambers, kitchens, and private bedrooms. The Akkadians either rebuilt or expanded temples throughout their empire. The city of Nippur, for example, featured temples to Enlil and Inanna in one large temple complex. The dominant feature of a temple complex was the ziggurat, a pyramid-shaped stepped building with a flat top. Ziggurats appeared in temple compounds throughout Mesopotamia.

Sculpture was a popular art form in the Akkadian period. The most popular types of sculptures were heads alone, statues of humans or gods, and bas-reliefs of major historical events. Two carved heads from Akkadian statues have survived from that time. The bronze head of a king, wearing a type of wig-helmet, may be a portrait of King Sargon. The other head, although worn, shows a very natural portrait of a man. Archaeologists do not know for certain whom the sculpture portrays, but many think it may be Sargon. Bas-relief sculptures honored the accomplishments of the military and of Akkadian kings in particular. While some of these bas-relief art works cover full walls, most are on stelae.

Ziggurats

A ziggurat was a large, flat-topped structure with a temple on top. The facades, or outer walls, were made from brick that had been baked in a special oven called a kiln. The inner core was made of unbaked brick. The temple's base was square or rectangular. Steps led up the sides of a ziggurat to a small sanctuary (the most holy part of a temple or church) on top of the building.

Public worship did not take place at the ziggurat. The building was considered a house of god. Priests who performed the rites (religious ceremonies) held in ziggurats may have been the only people allowed to attend the ceremonies.

The ziggurat walls sloped and the top was flat, much like a pyramid with the top cut off. In fact, a ziggurat is sometimes called a stepped pyramid. Priests may have reached the top of some ziggurats by a ramp or a stairway.

The shape of a ziggurat is like a mountain. Some researchers believe this shape represents a route to the gods. The shape might also have been chosen to symbolize the mountain that appears in many early Mesopotamian creation myths. Another possible idea is that the ziggurat was a bridge between heaven and earth. Whatever the reason for the shape, ziggurats were well built and about 30 have survived to this day.

These are the ruins of an ancient ziggurat in Ur, built around 2100 b.c.e.

The artistry of cylinder seal cutters reached a high point during the Akkadian Empire. Akkadian seal cutters produced signature seals with carefully spaced figures drawn in great detail. On many cylinder seals, the carvings are near-perfect miniatures of human and animal figures.

Akkad's capital, Agade, has never been found. Historians know it existed because it is mentioned in legends, contracts, tax documents, and other materials written at the time.

THE LAST AKKADIAN KINGS

Naram-Sin (r. ca. 2254–2218 B.C.E.) was the grandson of Sargon and the next ruler after Manishtusu. Naram-Sin was as well-known as his grandfather had been and became the hero of many Akkadian legends. Unfortunately, Naram-Sin was not the leader Akkad needed.

Stories told about Naram-Sin suggest that the king was an excellent military leader but not much admired by his people. He declared himself to be a god, which did not impress his people. He was the first king to be called the King of the Four Quarters, which covered all the land in the Fertile Crescent.

According to legend, the god Enlil gave the rule of the southern lands to Sargon. The goddess Inanna then set up a holy place in the temple in Agade. She filled the warehouses with food and grain so that the people would have food. She also set up a place especially for women. The kingdom of Akkad was at peace. Then, Naram-Sin became king and built up the walls of Agade as high as the sky. Naram-Sin tore the temple down, planning to build a new, better temple, even though Enlil had warned him not to do so. When Naram-Sin ignored the god, he was punished. Several city-states, including Elam and Marhashi (a city-state east of Elam), declared their independence from Akkad. Then the god sent the Gutians (or Guti) to attack Agade. The Gutians were warriors from the Zagros Mountains in the north. Enlil also brought drought to the land, which led to famine (a time when little food is available).

When Naram-Sin died, his son Shar-kali-sharri (r. ca. 2217–2193 B.C.E.) took his place. His name meant "king of all kings." The year his reign ended, the Gutians gained control of Agade. The Sumerian city of Ur also revolted against Akkadian rule and gained its independence. The Akkadians slowly lost power as other cultures took their place in Mesopotamia.

This map shows the Babylonian Empire during the Old Babylonian Period in ca. 1750 B.C.E., when the empire was ruled by Hammurabi. Hammurabi's territory included the cities of Larsa, Uruk, Babylon, Eshnunna, and Mari. During this period, the coastline of the Persian Gulf extended several miles further inland than it does today.

As the Akkadians lost power, another cultural group from the east, the Elamites, began conquering parts of Mesopotamia. The Elamites held Ur under siege. (A siege is when an army cuts off a town or fort from the outside so it cannot receive supplies and the inhabitants cannot escape.) In about 2004 B.C.E., the people of Ur were starving and were so desperate that they opened the city gates. The Elamites showed no pity. They slaughtered the people, looted homes and temples, and celebrated their victory by destroying most of the city's public buildings. The king of Ur, Ibbi-Sin (r. ca. 2028–2004 B.C.E.), was carried off as a captive.

THE RISE OF THE BABYLONIANS

From 2000 B.C.E. to 1900 B.C.E., the city-states in Mesopotamia often battled. No one city-state rose to become powerful and control large areas. In the midst of this confusion, a new group slipped into Mesopotamia

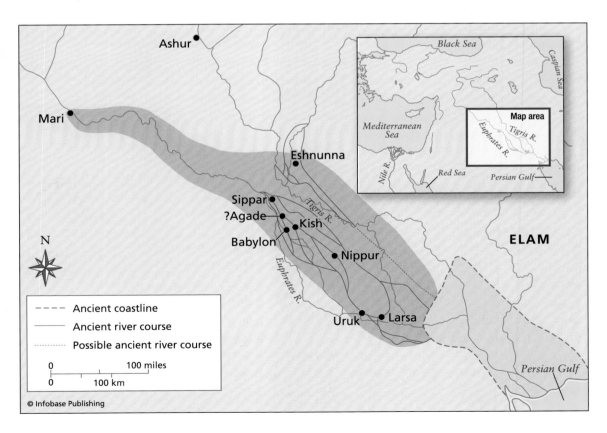

IN THEIR OWN WORDS

The Destruction of Ur

From 1922 to 1934, British archaeologist Charles Leonard Woolley (1880–1960) excavated the ruins of Ur. He uncovered royal tombs, a ziggurat, and temples to the gods of Ur. Many were decorated with inscriptions, including this one. It was written more than 4,000 years ago by an unidentified poet, who described the destruction of Ur by the Elamites. (*Potsherds* are broken pieces of ceramics, sometimes used to line roads.)

Dead men, not potsherds,
Covered the approaches,
The walls were gaping,
The high gates, the roads,

Were piled with the dead.
In the side streets, where feasting
*   crowds would gather,*
Scattered they lay.
In all the streets and roadways bodies
*   lay.*
In the open fields that used to fill with
*   dancers,*
They lay in heaps.
The country's blood now filled its hole,
Like metal in a mold;
Bodies dissolved—like fat left in the sun.

(Source: Nemet-Nejat, Karen Rhea. *Daily Life in Ancient Mesopotamia.* Westport, Conn.: Greenwood Press, 1998.)

and took over. These were the Amorites, people from present-day Syria. Like the Akkadians, they were a Semitic people and spoke a Semitic language.

The Amorites built a central government to control their lands, which included most of the land formerly ruled by Akkad and Sumer. They chose Babylon as their capital city, and it is from the name of this city that they have come to be known as the Babylonians.

The Amorites believed that their king was a god. As a result, the kings had tremendous power over their people. The people had to give the king whatever he demanded. Taxes were heavy, and everyone had to pay. Young men were all required to serve in the king's army. The empire ruled over many city-states, and those cities had no local power. Every resident was responsible to the king in Babylon, and any crime committed was considered a crime against the king's rule.

From about 1894 B.C.E. to 1595 B.C.E., Babylonia was under the rule of several native Babylonian kings. Five kings reigned and left barely a memory, until Hammurabi (r. ca. 1792–1750 B.C.E.), the sixth king

The Dig at Tell Hariri

The archaeological site of Tell Hariri, in modern-day Syria, is the site of an important city-state once known as Mari. (In archaeology, a *tell* is an artificial mound formed by the accumulated remains of ancient settlements.) It is located near the modern town of Abu Kamal on the western bank of the Euphrates River, near the border with Iraq.

Originally, Mari was ruled by Sumerian and then Akkadian kings. In 1761 B.C.E., it was conquered by the Babylonian king Hammurabi. Hammurabi raided the palace of King Zimri-Lim (r. ca. 1776–1761 B.C.E.), destroyed much of the city, and ordered the surrounding protective brick walls to be knocked down.

Mari became little more than a small village in the Babylonian Empire. The main part of the city was abandoned and, without protective walls, the city streets and buildings filled with dust and dirt.

Unknowingly, Hammurabi did history a great favor. The earth that filled Mari preserved the city for modern archaeologists. Finding Tell Hariri was an accident. In 1933, a group of Bedouins (a nomadic people who live in the desert regions of North Africa and the Middle East) was looking through a mound for a gravestone. They found, instead, a headless statue. Word of the find spread quickly, and the Louvre Museum in Paris, France, sent archaeologists to the site to begin their dig.

French archaeologist André Parrot (1901–1980) uncovered a palace that was remarkably well preserved. The rubble was removed inch by inch, revealing throne rooms, bathing rooms, bedrooms, and kitchens. According

of Babylonia. There are good records of Hammurabi's reign, and they indicate that he was regarded as an important king.

Hammurabi became king after the death of his father, Sin-muballit (r. ca. 1812–1793 B.C.E.). Hammurabi was fairly young when he became king, perhaps as young as 18 or 20. As with most Mesopotamian kings, he began his rule by going to war. In 1787 B.C.E., Hammurabi conquered Uruk, another powerful city-state. Over the next several years, Babylonia was at war with peoples from the northwest and the east, as Hammurabi attempted to expand his kingdom.

As the Babylonians became stronger, their enemies banded together to fight them. In the east, the city-states of Ashur, Eshnunna, and Elam joined forces in 1764 B.C.E. and pushed back a Babylonian

to Parrot, after cleaning the terra–cotta (clay) bathtubs, they were ready for use. Large pottery jars that once held oil, wine, and grain were found in the kitchen. The documents in Zimri-Lim's library included lists of groceries purchased for the palace inhabitants and a census of skilled craftsmen and tradesmen in Mari. One document encouraged Zimri-Lim to deal harshly with some unruly soldiers by cutting off the head of one of the worst offenders.

Tell Hariri provided archaeologists and historians with an accurate glimpse into the past. King Zimri-Lim's library yielded more than 20,000 clay documents that enabled historians to fix the dates of many Mesopotamian events.

Since 1933, Tell Hariri has been the scene of nearly continuous archaeological work. The dig requires a slow, methodical process of removing each layer of dirt, and less than half the area has been uncovered. It seems

Archaeologists have uncovered this throne room at the archaeological dig at Tell Hariri.

that every layer of earth removed from Tell Hariri reveals a new treasure to be studied.

Today, Tell Hariri is a United Nations World Heritage site. Its treasures can be found in the Louvre, and at museums in Aleppo and Damascus, in Syria.

advance on their territory. A year later, in 1763 B.C.E., Hammurabi came into conflict with the king of another city-state, Rim-Sin (r. ca. 1822–1763 B.C.E.) of Larsa. He used a new tactic to overwhelm Larsa. He dammed the Euphrates River and stopped the flow of water into the city. The people needed water to live, and they soon surrendered to Hammurabi's army. The army then overwhelmed several cities in southern Mesopotamia, destroying their fortress walls.

Over the next few years, the Babylonians were constantly at war with different cultures. War was one way to expand territory and to build a larger population under the king's rule. The larger the population was, the more tax money could be collected. The Babylonians also went to war to protect their territory against other invaders.

This bronze and gold figure originally showed Hammurabi praying before a sacred tree.

His success in Larsa encouraged Hammurabi to try the same tactic again. In 1755 B.C.E., he ordered the damming of the Tigris River and finally defeated the people of Eshnunna in the east.

Hammurabi was quite proud of his victories, which is shown in the artwork of the time. He had many bas-reliefs made honoring those victories. He announced to his people that he was not just king of Babylonia, but of the four regions (areas surrounding Babylonia, but not beyond the Taurus and Zagros Mountains in the north and east, the Persian Gulf and the Mediterranean Sea in the south and west) and all the people of Akkad and Sumer.

The king also liked to think of himself as a great builder. Perhaps his greatest accomplishments were the canals he built. The canal at Sippar connected the Tigris and the Euphrates. He built up Sippar for protection from his enemies and surrounded the city with a moat (a defensive ditch around a city or building that is usu-ally filled with water)—a very unusual idea in a land that was mostly dry. Hammurabi also built a great palace in Babylon and several temples.

But not all of Hammurabi's time was spent in wars of conquest. He made sure his armies had sufficient food and supplies, and he required his officials to provide lists of products made in their regions. To make sure they sent in accurate figures about how much grain was in the storehouses and sheep in the fields, Hammurabi sent more officials to double-check all the reports. Yet Hammurabi's most important contribution was a list of laws that everyone was required to follow.

HAMMURABI'S LAWS

Under the Babylonians, laws became clearly defined for perhaps the first time. The government wrote down descriptions of what was considered crime and how it was to be punished. Government officials actively pursued criminals, and their punishments became public events. The most common punishment was death. There was a long list of crimes that carried the death penalty, including such crimes as behaving badly in a tavern or inn.

The Babylonian king most closely associated with this new legal system was Hammurabi. In 1755 B.C.E., he set down a list of laws that has influenced all lawmaking since. While a list of laws might not seem important, it was a critical step in the development of civilization. For the first time, everyone followed the same laws. Before that, every governor made his own laws. The governor could favor friends by allowing them to get away with crimes, or punish enemies by giving out harsh sentences for minor crimes.

Under Hammurabi's code of laws, crimes and the punishments they carried were listed in detail. Hammurabi said he created this list of laws so that everyone in his empire would have a chance to get justice. He wrote, "Let a man who has been wronged and has a cause, go before my stele . . . and let him have my words inscribed on the monument read out" (quoted in Don Nardo's *Ancient Mesopotamia*). Most people could not read and needed a scribe to read out the laws, but they could still take advantage of the legal process. If ordinary people had been wronged, they could go to the government and be treated the same way as a noble or a priest would be treated.

Hammurabi's code of laws lists 282 laws and punishments. The laws covered some areas that people today consider to be private (such as family relations), and the punishments were harsh. But in 1755 B.C.E., when the code of laws was published, most people believed the punishments fit the crimes. If a person caused someone to lose an eye, the convicted person lost an eye as punishment. Murder, robbery, and kidnapping were punished by death. A person who falsely accused someone of a serious crime, such as murder, was put to death. Other death-penalty crimes included receiving stolen goods, breaking into a home, arson (deliberately setting a fire), sorcery (witchcraft), and doing a government job badly.

Laws of the Gods

Hammurabi claimed the idea to make a formal legal code was brought to him by the gods. In the introduction to his code of laws, he stated, "[A]t that time, the gods Anu [An] and Bel [Enlil], for the enhancement of the well-being of the people, named me by my name, Hammurabi, the pious prince, who venerates the gods, to make justice prevail in the land, to abolish the wicked and the evil, to prevent the strong from oppressing the weak; to rise like the sun-god Shamash [Utu] over all humankind, to illuminate the land" (quoted in *Law Collections from Mesopotamia and Asia Minor*). Saying these ideas came from the gods gave them even greater authority.

The Code of Hammurabi is engraved on this stele, which is seven feet, five inches high and was made in the first half of the 18th century B.C.E. The top portion shows Hammurabi with Shamash [Utu], the sun god. Shamash is presenting to Hammurabi a staff and ring, which symbolize the power to administer the law.

IN THEIR OWN WORDS

Hammurabi's Code of Laws

These are just a few of the 282 laws in Hammurabi's code. (A *shekel* is a unit of money. *Covet* means to desire to have something.)

If a man steals valuables belonging to the god or the palace, that man shall be killed, and also he who received the stolen goods from him shall be killed.

If a man steals an ox, a sheep, a donkey, a pig, or a boat—if it belongs either to the god or to the palace, he shall give thirtyfold; if it belongs to a commoner, he shall replace it tenfold; if the thief does not have anything to give, he shall be killed.

If a man should enable a palace slave, a palace slave woman, a commoner's slave, or a commoner's slave woman to leave through the main city-gate, he shall be killed.

If a man seizes a fugitive slave or slave woman in the open country and leads him

back to his owner, the slave owner shall give him two shekels of silver.

If a fire breaks out in a man's house, and a man who came to help put it out covets the household furnishings belonging to the householder, and takes the household furnishings belonging to the householder, that man shall be cast into that very fire.

If a man has a debt lodged against him, and the storm-god Adad devastates his field or a flood sweeps away the crops, or there is no grain grown in the field that year due to insufficient water—in that year he will not repay grain to his creditor; he shall suspend performance of his contract and he will not give interest payments for that year.

If a commoner should strike the cheek of another commoner, he shall weigh and deliver 10 shekels of silver.

(Source: Roth, Martha T., et al. *Law Collections from Mesopotamia and Asia Minor*, Atlanta: Scholars Press, 1995, reprint 1997.)

Crimes that did not merit the death penalty still carried serious punishments. It was common for criminals to be burned or branded with a hot piece or metal, whipped, or have their property taken. Some criminals were sent into exile (forced to leave one's homeland) with no money or goods—which was almost the same as killing them, since they were unlikely to survive. Others lost an eye, tongue, or nose, or had an arm or leg broken. Breaking the law in Hammurabi's day was very serious.

Military power and religion combined to make Babylonia a powerful empire. After Hammurabi died, five more native Babylonian kings ruled before this first era of Babylonian power came to an end.

CHAPTER 3

THE FINAL YEARS OF POWER

IN MESOPOTAMIA, THE POLITICAL LANDSCAPE WAS ALWAYS changing. Cultures would rise to power and then fall, sometimes quickly and sometimes slowly. As they weakened, other cultures would become stronger and take their place. The reasons for war never changed. Kings grew greedy for power, land, and wealth. The easiest way to acquire all three was to conquer a neighboring city-state.

In 1600 B.C.E., the Babylonians were becoming weaker while a group called the Hittites was gaining power. The Hittites were an Indo-European people (people originated in Australia, Iran, or the Eurasian steppes) from outside Mesopotamia. They came from the north, although no one knows exactly where their culture began. When they invaded Mesopotamia in about 1600 B.C.E., they found much in the existing culture that they liked and kept. They also brought many changes.

THE HITTITES

The Hittite Empire was at its strongest from about 1600 to 1200 B.C.E. The Hittites carried on an increasing number of wars to acquire more land. Over time, they controlled Anatolia and Syria and began moving into Egypt. The Egyptians, however, thought the Hittites were a savage people. They fiercely resisted Hittite conquest.

The Hittite king served as the political head, military leader, and supreme judge. He also represented the Hittite storm god. When the king died, he himself became a god. The Hittite economy was based on farming. Nobles—mainly the king—owned the land, and the common people were freemen, skilled craftsmen, or slaves. The heart of the

OPPOSITE
This statue of King Ashurnasirpal II was placed in the Temple of Ishtar. It was designed to remind the goddess Ishtar that the king was very religious.

45

Part of a bronze Hittite battle-axe. This is the part that was opposite the blade.

Hittite empire was in present-day Anatolia, Turkey. The area was rich in metals, especially silver and iron. During the empire period, the Hittites developed iron-working technology.

Smelting iron was the most important skill the Hittites brought to Mesopotamia. Smelting iron means extracting the metal from crude ore (a mixture of metal and rock). The Hittites knew how to work iron, melt it, pound the metal into tools, and temper the iron (make it stronger) by heating it and then plunging it into cold water. The Hittites made tools and weapons that were stronger and longer lasting than the copper and bronze tools used in Mesopotamia at the time. Their knives stayed sharper longer.

The Hittites used their iron-working skills to produce weapons of war that helped them defeat other empires. Working iron was a skill that the Hittites did not want to share, because it helped them maintain their power. However, as the empire began to lose power after 1200 B.C.E., the secret of Hittite iron-making became common knowledge.

One positive effect the Hittites had on Mesopotamia was increasing trade. The Hittite Empire traded far beyond the boundaries of the Tigris and the Euphrates Rivers. The empire ruled over most of present-day Turkey, parts of Syria, and south along the coast of the Mediterranean Sea. Trade routes stretched south onto the Arabian Peninsula and east into modern Iran.

The Hittites brought new products and ideas into Mesopotamia. They also carried Mesopotamian culture, such as foods, customs, and language, beyond the region. Many of the inventions and advances developed by the Sumerians reached into Hittite lands and were traded along Hittite trading routes.

In Mesopotamia, the Hittites thought that Hammurabi's code and the other laws that had been added to it were somewhat brutal. While they agreed that many specific actions should be declared illegal, they did not agree with the punishments. Under the Old Babylonian legal system, criminals could expect to lose a body part or their lives for most crimes. Under the new Hittite laws, criminals

A Hittite Story

Like all the cultures of the time, the Hittites told myths and legends about their gods and heroes, and about the world around them. The story of the god Telepinu explains the arrival of spring.

Once, the god Telepinu became angry because the world had become so evil. His mind was so filled with anger that he walked away with his sandals on the wrong feet. This act made the earth dry up, plants die, and animals fail to produce young. The world's human beings were starving, and many died of hunger.

Seeing how bad the situation was on earth, the sun god called together all the other gods to search for Telepinu. They looked all over, but they could not find him. The goddess of heaven suggested they send a bee to find Telepinu. The other gods laughed. What could a bee do that they could not?

The bee flew and flew until it was nearly exhausted, but finally found Telepinu asleep. To wake the sleeping Telepinu, the bee stung him. Telepinu woke up angrier than he was before. He began destroying everything he saw. The bee asked the gods to send an eagle to carry Telepinu to where the gods were waiting.

Kamrusepa, the goddess of magic, then eased Telepinu's mind with cream. She sweetened his disposition with honey. She washed his body with oil and eased his anger with ointment. Telepinu grew calm. The earth returned to normal. People cleaned their homes and prepared for the New Year. Spring arrived and life began again. The people hung lambskins in the temple to remind them that after the cold of anger comes the warmth of new life.

paid fines. Murder carried a huge fine, but there were few crimes that carried the death penalty.

THE KASSITES

At the same time that the Hittites ruled Anatolia and Syria, another people gained power in Mesopotamia. They were the Kassites, and no one is quite sure of their exact origins.

During the Babylonian Empire, the Kassites came to Mesopotamia to work the fields. Agriculture required many workers, and foreigners who moved to the area to farm were welcome. The Kassites held power in Babylonia from about 1570 B.C.E. to 1170 B.C.E.

CONNECTIONS

Settling Differences by Treaty

One of the new ideas the Hittites brought to Mesopotamia was treaties. In the past, all disputes with other nations, kingdoms, or cultures were settled by wars. The winner conquered the loser and imposed their will.

The Hittites had a different idea. In 1284 B.C.E., after several battles, the Hittite's King Hattusili III (r. ca. 1265–1235 B.C.E) and King Ramesses II (r. ca. 1279–1212 B.C.E.) of Egypt signed a treaty to resolve their differences. They agreed to stop fighting against each other and to honor each other's national borders. They also agreed to support each other if a third party attacked either one. This was a new idea, and one that is used today by nations that form alliances.

The Kassites built themselves a new capital in the heart of Mesopotamia that they called Dur-Kurigalzu, west of modern-day Baghdad. They held a large amount of land between the Tigris and the Euphrates Rivers.

However, a few years after the Hittites sacked Babylon in 1595 B.C.E., the Kassites gained control under King Agum II Kakrime (r. ca. 1595–1545 B.C.E.). Agum II Kakrime is credited with bringing statues of the god Marduk and Marduk's goddess wife, Zarpanit, back to Babylon's temples in about 1570 B.C.E. According to legend, the first Kassite king, Gandash (r. ca. 1730–1705 B.C.E.), took away these important statues when he invaded Babylon during his reign. His invasion was crushed, but he managed to get away with the statues. Their return meant a great deal to the Babylonians. After the statues were recovered, they were returned to the temple. It was also said that Agum II Kakrime encouraged the Kassites to follow the social customs of the Babylonians and accept their gods and religion.

This was a time of great change in Mesopotamia. People from southeastern Europe began arriving in the region, as did people from India and the Far East. People now traveled by horse-drawn chariots and carts, which increased the speed of travel. Empires struggled to keep control of the lands they held for the same reason earlier kings had struggled: There were always other rulers who wanted more wealth, power, and land.

THE RISE OF THE ASSYRIANS

Gaining and losing power was an endless cycle in ancient Mesopotamia. As the Hittites and Kassites began to lose power, another culture rose to take their place. This new empire was the Assyrian Empire. At

A King of Wisdom and Prudence

This inscription, preserved in an Assyrian copy, was originally deposited in the temple at Babylon by Kassite king Agum II Kakrime. It describes his achievements on behalf of the god Marduk and his spouse, Zarpanit. But first, the king declares his own greatness by pointing out his relationship to the gods and his royal titles. (A *scion* is an heir or younger family member.)

> *I am Agumkakrime, the son of Tashshi-gurumash; the illustrious descendant of god Shuqamuna; called by Anu and Bel, Ea and Marduk, Sin and Shamash; the powerful hero of Ishtar, the warrior among the goddesses.*

> *I am a king of wisdom and prudence; a king who grants hearing and pardon; the son of Tashshigurumash; the descendant of Abirumash, the crafty warrior; the first son among the numerous family of the great Agum; an illustrious, royal scion who holds the reins of the nation [and is] a mighty shepherd. . . .*

> *I am king of the country of Kashshu and of the Akkadians; king of the wide country of Babylon, who settles the numerous people in Ashnunak; the King of Padan and Alman; the King of Gutium, a foolish nation; [a king] who makes obedient to him the four regions, and has always been a favorite of the great gods.*

(Source: Guisepi, Robert A. "Ancient Sumeria," Available online. URL: http://history-world. org/sumeria.htm. Accessed March 21, 2008.)

the height of their power, the Assyrians ruled over all of Mesopotamia and parts of Persia (Iran), modern-day Jordan and Israel, and parts of Egypt.

Historians divide the Assyrian Empire into three periods: the Old Assyrian Period (1906–1392 B.C.E.), the Middle Assyrian Period (1392–1014 B.C.E.), and the Neo-Assyrian Period (911–609 B.C.E.).

The king who laid the foundations of the Assyrian Empire was Ashur-uballit I (r. ca. 1365–1330 B.C.E.). He threw off control by the Mittani kingdom, which ruled the area between the Hittites and Kassites in northeast Syria. Ashur-uballit I established firm control over his territory. But he did not seek to expand his empire, and for nearly 200 years the Assyrians, Kassites, and Hittites lived peacefully.

When Tukulti-Ninurta I (r. ca. 1244–1208 B.C.E.) became the Assyrian king, he brought a new vision of what Assyria could become. He wanted Assyria to rule over all of Mesopotamia. He was a skilled military leader, and he took his army across the Euphrates to attack the Hittites. Records of his military victories claim that Tukulti-Ninurta took more than 28,000 Hittite prisoners in his campaigns.

The king also rebuilt much of the capital of Ashur and founded a new city called Kar-Tukulti-Ninurta on the other side of the Tigris River in modern-day Iraq. Building the new city cost so much that his people rebelled. The king was thrown into prison in his palace. The palace was burned to the ground, and, history notes, the leader of the rebellion was Tukulti-Ninurta's son and Assyria's future king, Ashur-nadin-apli (r. ca. 1207–1203 B.C.E.).

ASSYRIA'S GREATEST ERA

The Middle Assyrian Period's greatest leader was Tiglathpileser I (r. ca. 1115–1077 B.C.E.), a strong military leader. This king was responsible for increasing Assyrian territory in Mesopotamia. Tiglathpileser was a good administrator and an avid hunter. He also had an interest in animals; when he was king, he founded several zoos in Assyria.

Tiglathpileser began rebuilding Assyria's farm-based economy, which had been ignored for years. Fruit, vegetables, and grains raised in Assyria were brought to cities to be traded. Extra grain was stored so that the people would be fed even if there were a crop failure. The king established trade agreements with the Phoenicians, a culture that lived along the coast of the Mediterranean Sea in modern-day Lebanon and Syria. The Phoenicians were sea travelers, and they brought many products from other cultures on the Mediterranean. These traders carried wood, slaves, glass, and purple dye to Assyrian markets. They also brought silver, tin, and other metals to Mesopotamia.

Because he was a military leader, Tiglathpileser built a strong, skilled army. He led his army against tribes living in the Zagros Mountains and against the Aramaeans who lived to the southwest in modern-day Syria. He took over land from the Aramaeans that reached as far as the Mediterranean. This enabled the king to build up trade routes to the west.

ASHURNASIRPAL II

The first of the great Assyrian kings of the Neo-Assyrian Period was Ashurnasirpal II, who reigned from about 884 to 859 B.C.E. He began by building a new capital at Nimrud (a place the king called Calah), located south of Nineveh on the Tigris River. He wanted to get away from the old city of Ashur where so many kings had ruled and died and build a new capital city.

Building a new city required thousands of workers, as well as massive amounts of brick, stone, marble, metal, and gemstones. It took years to build the five miles of walls needed to protect the new city. A new canal had to be dug to bring water for the city's residents and to irrigate crops in the fields. Within the city, a temple complex took up a large portion of the area, as did a magnificent new palace.

The city may have been magnificent, but collecting the wealth to build it made enemies of all the people Ashurnasirpal conquered.

IN THEIR OWN WORDS

The Banquet of Ashurnasirpal II

King Ashurnasirpal II built himself a magnificent palace in the capital city he called Calah. The city and palace were made from the best building materials available at the time. Ashurnasirpal explains how, after removing the rubble of a city that was once on the same land, he built his great palace.

I dug down to the water level; I heaped up a [new] terrace from the water level to the upper edge [measuring] 120 layers of bricks; upon that I erected as my royal seat and for my personal enjoyment seven beautiful halls [roofed with] boxwood, Magan-ash, cedar, cypress, juniper, boxwood . . . . I surrounded them [the doors] with decorative bronze bolts; to proclaim my heroic deeds, I painted on walls with vivid blue paint how I have marched across the mountain ranges, the foreign countries and the seas, my conquests in all countries. . . .

When the palace was ready for use, Ashurnasirpal held a magnificent banquet. He ordered the following to be prepared for his guests.

1,000 fattened head of cattle, 1,000 calves, 10,000 stable sheep, 15,000 lambs . . . 1,000 spring lambs, 500 stags, 500 gazelles, 1,000 ducks, 500 geese, 500 kurku-geese. . . .

When I inaugurated the palace at Calah, I treated for ten days with food and drink 47,074 persons, men and women, who were bid to come from across my entire country. . . . I did them due honors and sent them back, healthy and happy, to their own countries.

(Source: "The Banquet of Ashurnasirpal II." Wittenburg University. Available online. URL: http://www4.wittenberg.edu/academics/hist/dbrookshedstrom/105/bqtashur.htm. Accessed March 21, 2008.)

The Assyrian army became known for reaching levels of brutality and cruelty that were horrifying, even among people who lived with nearly continuous war.

Here is just one example of Ashurnasirpal's brutality. In 881 B.C.E., Ashurnasirpal began a campaign against the rebel governor of Nishtun. Within a year, the governor of Nishtun was captured and publicly whipped. Two years later, one of Ashurnasirpal's loyal followers was killed by rebels. The king's troops attacked quickly and defeated the rebels who had killed Ashurnasirpal's loyal men. Tablets recorded Ashurnasipal's treatment of those who had opposed him. "Many of the captives taken, I burned in a fire. Many I took alive; from some I cut off their hands to the wrist, from others, I cut off their noses, ears, and fingers, I put out the eyes of many of the soldiers. I burnt their young men and women to death" (quoted in Dale M. Brown's *Mesopotamia: The Mighty Kings*).

SHALMANESER III

When Ashurnasirpal II died, he was followed by his son Shalmaneser III (r. ca. 858–824 B.C.E.). Shalmaneser enjoyed a long reign that was marked by continuous wars against tribes of the eastern mountains, the Babylonians, the Syrians, and the Egyptians. There were few national groups that Shalmaneser was not willing to meet on the battlefield. In fact, Shalmaneser spent 31 of his 34 years as king going to war.

In 853 B.C.E., the Syrians formed an alliance with several other enemies of the Assyrians. They met on the battlefield in Qarqar (in modern-day Syria), but the Syrian alliance suffered serious losses. Like his father, Shalmaneser had tablets recorded with warnings about how he treated his enemies. "I slew 14,000 of their warriors with the sword. I rained destruction upon them. The plain was too small to let their bodies fall; the wide countryside was used up in burying them. With their corpses, I spanned the Orontes [River] as with a bridge" (from Brown's *Mesopotamia: The Mighty Kings*). When Shalmaneser stated that "I" slew 14,000 warriors, he was referring to the total deaths caused by his soldiers. He also claimed that the Assyrians captured hundreds of horses and chariots, but it is impossible to know if this is an exaggeration.

During Shalmaneser's reign, the Assyrians defeated the Syrians to the west. They also invaded ancient Israel. Shalmaneser filled his treasury with wealth from conquered nations. But despite the military

The Discovery of Nimrud

Sometimes, archaeologists are just lucky. In 1957, British archaeologist Max Mallowan (1904–1978) decided to take a walk to get away from the dig where he was working. He and a fellow archaeologist wandered away aimlessly. Mallowan spotted a brick and picked it up. The brick bore the name Shalmaneser III, written in cuneiform.

Mallowan and his associates began digging and uncovered one of the greatest archaeological finds of all time: the royal palace of Shalmaneser. The dig at Nimrud has uncovered thousands of artifacts that tell the story of Assyria during Shalmaneser's reign.

This bas-relief shows a warrior. It was found at Nimrud, in the palace of Shalmaneser III.

victories and the wealth they brought in, Shalmaneser's people were not happy with their ruler. They suffered under high taxes and endless military campaigns. The king's long reign saw many revolts and countless efforts to overthrow Assyrian rule.

Shalmaneser built a palace that was even greater than his father's. Shalmaneser's palace was twice the size of the first palace of Nimrud. It covered more than 12 acres and had more than 200 rooms.

Shalmaneser had several sons. In 828 B.C.E., one of them—Ashur-daninpal (dates unknown)—convinced the nobles and leaders of 27 Assyrian cities to revolt against his father. By this time, Shalmaneser was an old man. He decided to send his son Shamshi-Adad V (r. ca. 824–811 B.C.E.) to meet the rebels on the battlefield. The fighting lasted three years. Finally, in 824 B.C.E., Shalmaneser died. Shamshi-Adad had won both the battle and the kingship.

SARGON II

A new Assyrian dynasty began when Sargon II (r. ca. 722–705 B.C.E.) seized power from the previous king, Shalmaneser V (r. ca. 727–722 B.C.E.). Sargon II chose his name because it means "true king." Sargon II modeled his rule after Sargon I of Akkad, who was considered one of Mesopotamia's greatest kings.

He immediately divided Assyria into 70 provinces, each with its own governor or viceroy. The governors reported to Sargon II and were responsible for keeping peace, collecting taxes, and providing soldiers for the king's army.

In an effort to win his people's support, Sargon II tried to make an alliance with yet another invading people, the Chaldeans. The Chaldeans lived along the northern coast of the Persian Gulf. During this period, kings formed alliances with other cultures. These alliances or treaties served several purposes: An ally provided soldiers if any member of the alliance was attacked by an enemy, and one ally did not attack another.

The Assyrians had once been at war with the Chaldeans. When Sargon II signed a treaty with the Chaldeans, his people knew that the Chaldeans would no longer be their enemies. He also announced that people living in Ashur and Harran did not have to pay taxes. This act may have been popular with people in Ashur and Harran, but it angered Assyrians living in other cities.

Unfortunately, the alliance with the Chaldeans proved to be a bad idea. The Chaldeans also made an alliance with yet another invading force, the Elamites. Together, the Elamites and the Chaldeans conquered Babylonia. Suddenly, Sargon found himself in the position of having to defend his empire, build an army, and protect his people.

In 720 B.C.E., Sargon II led his army against the Elamite king Ummanigash (r. ca. 720s B.C.E.) and the Chaldeans. The Assyrians lost the battle. But Sargon II was an ambitious king who wanted more land and more power, and he was not about to give up. He led his people against the Syrians at Qarqar and gained control of the Syrian cities of Damascus, Arpad, and Simirra. Sargon II then turned his eyes southward and began a campaign to conquer Gaza and Rafah (both in present-day Gaza Strip). He battled and defeated Egyptian troops in this area.

War continued as Sargon II expanded his hold over an ever-increasing amount of territory. His holdings reached south nearly to Egypt, west to the Mediterranean Sea, and into the Zagros Mountains to the east. As is typical of battles at the time, the results were recorded in the number of soldiers slain, prisoners taken, and gold and silver won. In a battle in 714 B.C.E. against King Rusas of Urartu, a kingdom near the Caucasus Mountains, Sargon's men are said to have destroyed 430 villages. They looted the temples of the Urartan people, taking more than one ton of gold and five tons of silver. The losses in men were great on the Urartan side, but Sargon claimed to have lost only one charioteer, two horsemen, and three members of the royal court. However, this is probably an exaggeration. The Assyrians did burn villages and loot temples, but it is likely that they suffered many more losses than they admitted to.

Warfare has always been expensive. Soldiers needed horses, chariots, weapons, clothing, and food. They also expected to be paid.

This massive sculpture of a bull with wings and a human head stood at the gate of Sargon II's palace in Dur-Sharrukin. The sculpture is about 13 feet deep and 13 feet tall, and about 3.25 feet across.

Even the massive amounts of gold and silver looted from the defeated enemies would not have been enough to keep such a large army supplied and housed. Therefore, Sargon, like the kings before him, taxed his people.

But war was not the only reason for taxes. Despite having excellent palaces available in Ashur and Nimrud, Sargon ordered the building of a new palace and city that would be called Dur-Sharrukin, or the Fortress of Sargon. The new town (located in modern Khorsabad) was rectangular and had to be built from scratch. Such a building project required the efforts of thousands of workers. In 706 B.C.E., the royal court moved into Dur-Sharrukin, even though the building was not yet complete. The following year, Sargon died in a battle against the Cimmerians, a nomadic people from the south of Russia.

CONNECTIONS

Sennacherib in the Bible

One of the kingdoms Sennacherib attacked was known as Judaea (or Judah). It was ruled by King Hezekiah, whose capital was Jerusalem. The defeat of Hezekiah is one of the many events in Mesopotamian history that is mentioned in the Bible. Sennacherib laid siege to the city of Jerusalem. Then he demanded a huge payment or else the Assyrians would destroy Jerusalem. Hezekiah had little choice but to pay. This excerpt from Second Kings, chapter 18, verses 13 to 16 (from *The Jewish Study Bible*) describes the ransom. In it, Hezekiah says he has done wrong because he has sinned against God.

In the 14th year of King Hezekiah, King Sennacherib of Assyria marched against all the fortified towns of Judah and seized them. King Hezekiah sent this message to the king of Assyria at Lachish: "I have done wrong; withdraw from me, and I shall bear whatever you impose on me." So the king of Assyria imposed upon King Hezekiah of Judah a payment of 300 talents of silver and 30 talents of gold. Hezekiah gave him all the silver that was on hand in the House of the Lord and in the treasuries of the palace. At that time Hezekiah cut down the doors and doorposts of the Temple of the Lord, which King Hezekiah had overlaid [with gold], and gave them to the king of Assyria.

As luck would have it, Sennacherib had to cut short his campaign against the kingdom of Judaea. An epidemic swept through his troops, killing nearly 185,000 men. With the size of his army drastically reduced, Sennacherib had to retreat. As the tale is told in the Bible, though, Judaea was spared because Hezekiah renewed his faith in God.

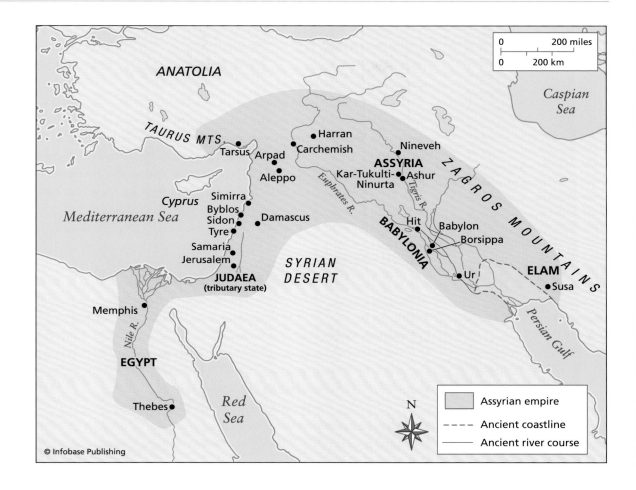

Sargon's plan at the beginning of his rule was to offer peace and prosperity to his people. But the constant forces of change in Mesopotamia made him into a king like all the Assyrian kings before him. He brought endless war and taxes to his people, built a city in his own honor, and conquered other nations. Under Sargon II, the Assyrians spread their power into the south. They conquered Judaea and captured Samaria in 717 B.C.E. after a three-year siege. The native people of the region were forced to leave.

SENNACHERIB

Sennacherib (r. ca. 705–ca. 681 B.C.E.) was an intelligent and gifted ruler, although, like his father, Sargon II, and other kings before him, he spent a lot of money. The capital city of Dur-Sharrukin had barely been

At its height in the mid-seventh century B.C.E., the Assyrian Empire covered much of Mesopotamia as well as the Levant, northern Egypt, and parts of western Iran and southern Turkey. Its principal cities, Ashur, from which Assyria took its name, and Nineveh, were located in Assyria's core region in northeastern Mesopotamia.

finished when Sennacherib decided to move to Ashur, the traditional capital of Assyria. Then, in 701 B.C.E., Nineveh became the Assyrian capital for the remainder of Sennacherib's reign. Every move cost an incredible amount of money.

The story of Sennacherib is much like the stories of other kings of Assyria. He fought battles and tried to increase the size of his empire. Also much like the stories of other kings, he was murdered by his children. In 681 B.C.E., Sennacherib was praying in the temple of Nergal when two of his sons attacked and killed him. Another son, Esarhaddon (r. ca. 681–669 B.C.E.) went after his brothers to avenge his father, but they escaped.

ESARHADDON

When Esarhaddon became king, the Assyrian Empire covered most of the present-day Middle East. But he wanted more land, power, and wealth. In his own words, Esarhaddon said, "I besieged, I captured, I plundered, I destroyed, I devastated, I burned with fire, I hung the heads of the kings upon the shoulders of their nobles and with singing and music I paraded" (quoted in R. C. Thomson's *The Prisms of Esarhaddon and Ashurbanipal Found at Nineveh, 1927-8*). It is easy to see why Esarhaddon was greatly feared by his enemies.

Over the next few years, Esarhaddon made war against an increasing number of his neighbors. He attacked Egypt, Sidon, and parts of Palestine, leaving destruction behind him. The city of Sidon was razed (completely destroyed), and Esarhaddon ordered that the head of Sidon's king be cut off. Then he looted the riches of Sidon, sending home chests filled with gold, silver, gems, ivory, maple, boxwood, and clothing made of wool and linen.

In Egypt, Esarhaddon conquered city after city, moving down the Nile River toward the lands of Ethiopia. He claimed, "I conquered Egypt, Upper Egypt, and Ethiopia . . . Tirhakah, its king, five times I fought with him with my javelin [a thrown spear] and I brought all of this land under my sway, I ruled it" (quoted in D. D. Luckenbill's *Records of Assyria*).

Long before he became king, Esarhaddon was married and had children. Children were very useful to a king. One of the sons would inherit the throne, and his daughters could be married to other rulers to ensure alliances and keep peace between Assyria and other

Ashurbanipal's army battles the Elamites in this stone relief.

nations. For example, one of Esarhaddon's daughters was married to a Scythian prince.

Esarhaddon wanted his son Sin-iddina-apla to inherit the throne after him, but the prince died in 672 B.C.E. Another son, Ashurbanipal, became the new heir to the throne, but other nobles and Assyrian priests despised him. They favored Shamash-shum-ukin. Esarhaddon had to use his power to persuade the members of his court to accept

Ashurbanipal. Contracts were written and signed ensuring their loyalty to Ashurbanipal.

By 670 B.C.E., Esarhaddon had his hands full trying to rule a vast empire and keep peace among the nobles of his court. He believed that many nobles were plotting against him, and reacted by having them killed. When he died the following year, Ashurbanipal became king of Assyria. Esarhaddon's other son, Shamash-shum-ukin became king of Babylonia, which was under the rule of the Assyrian Empire.

ASHURBANIPAL

Members of the royal Assyrian court may have hated Ashurbanipal (r. ca. 669–627 B.C.E.), but he is often considered the last great ruler of Assyria. When Ashurbanipal became king, Assyria's power stretched from modern-day Turkey to Iran, and westward far into Egypt. The new king chose Nineveh as his capital. Ashurbanipal did not remove

Ashurbanipal's Library

Ashurbanipal collected between 20,000 and 30,000 cuneiform tablets in his library. Although this was not the first library ever gathered, it was, perhaps, the most important. Sumerian, Akkadian, Babylonian, and Assyrian texts from the time were stored in this library, including the epic poem *Gilgamesh,* the best-known epic poem from Mesopotamia.

While Ashurbanipal's empire is long gone, his magnificent library still exists. It was uncovered at Nineveh by archaeologists in 1852. This library has yielded much of the information that is known about ancient Mesopotamia, including a nearly complete list of the rulers of the region.

The actual library was spread through several rooms and was organized by subject matter, much like today's public libraries. Rooms were devoted to science, poetry, religion, government, and geography. The information included legends, poems, and tales of greatness, but there were also government papers, information about military campaigns, and the secrets that spies found and relayed to their ruler. The library also had several scribes who served as librarians and were dedicated to adding to Ashurbanipal's collection.

local leaders and replace them with Assyrian leaders. He kept officials in conquered lands in their positions of authority.

Almost as soon as he became king, Egypt rebelled against Assyrian rule. Ashurbanipal sent troops to Egypt to regain control. This situation was repeated again five years later, until, in 654 B.C.E., the Assyrians were finally driven out of Egypt. The two nations, however, set up a trade agreement. This relationship probably was better for Assyria than ruling Egypt had been. Egypt was too far away from the Assyrian capital for a ruler to be able to maintain control. In addition, the Egyptians rebelled against all outside rule. Ruling Egypt from far away was expensive, but trade with Egypt would be profitable.

It was through Ashurbanipal's influence that his brother Shamash-shum-ukin became king of Babylonia. Unfortunately, Shamash-shum-ukin decided that Babylonia was not enough for him, and revolted against Ashurbanipal. Shamash-shum-ukin and his allies—Aramaeans, Elamites, and Arabs—rebelled in 652 B.C.E., but Ashurbanipal's army was stronger. Ashurbanipal laid siege to Babylon and nearby Borsippa. After two years, he defeated his brother, who then committed suicide.

But Ashurbanipal's greatest accomplishment did not take place on the battlefield. In addition to being a military leader, he was also highly educated. He had read many Sumerian and Akkadian legends, and took an interest in the culture of his empire. To preserve this culture, the king founded a well-stocked, well-organized library—the first in Mesopotamia.

Ashurbanipal's rule came to an end with his death in 627 B.C.E. Assyria's power weakened and the empire slowly dwindled. Assyria's enemies had become more powerful, and repeated raids on Assyrian cities left its people enslaved, its wealth stolen, and its might in ruins. A new empire—the Babylonian Empire—was on the rise.

THE NEO-BABYLONIAN PERIOD

The end of the Assyrians saw a rise in the power of the Babylonians. This was not an abrupt switch from one culture to the next. It was, instead, a gradual rise of one culture as the other culture began to weaken.

In Babylon, Nebuchadnezzar II (r. ca. 604–562 B.C.E.) came to power. His name means "Nebo who protects the crown." Nebuchad-

Which Babylonians?

Historians divide the Babylonian Empire into three periods because the power of the Babylonians rose and fell three times. The Old Babylonian Period flourished from about 1900 to 1595 B.C.E., and ruled over land lying between the Tigris and Euphrates Rivers. During this period, Hammurabi gave the Babylonians a code of law. During the Middle Babylonian Period (1595–1000 B.C.E.), or Kassite period, southern Mesopotamia became a stable and unified state. The Neo-Babylonian Period (625–539 B.C.E.) saw the end of Babylonian reign in Mesopotamia when the Persian king, Cyrus the Great, invaded Mesopotamia from the east.

nezzar was a Chaldean and the son of King Nabu-apla-usur (r. ca. 625–605 B.C.E.), who founded the Chaldean dynasty. Nabu-apla-usur took part in the invasion of Assyria by the Medes and the Babylonians in 614 B.C.E. Their combined efforts forced the Assyrians to retreat into northwestern Mesopotamia. This made room for the rise of the Neo-Babylonians.

Nebuchadnezzar II participated in many military campaigns. However, Nebuchadnezzar was as much a builder as a destroyer. He rebuilt old religious monuments and improved canals carrying water from the Euphrates. To protect his people, he surrounded Babylon with a double wall 10 miles long. The main entrance to the city featured an elaborate gate called the Ishtar Gate. Named for the goddess Ishtar (Inanna), the Ishtar Gate was another of Nebuchadnezzar's great accomplishments. It was decorated with beautiful dragons, bulls, and other creatures.

Nebuchadnezzar's many military conquests included destroying Jerusalem in 586 B.C.E. He captured Jerusalem's citizens and took them to Babylon. This time is referred to in Jewish history as the Babylonian Captivity.

IN THEIR OWN WORDS

Building the Ishtar Gate

This inscription was carved onto glazed brick on the walls of the Ishtar Gate in Babylon in about 600 B.C.E. It was written in Akkadian, and explains how and why the king rebuilt the gate entrance. Like many other inscriptions of kings throughout the ages, the text boasts about the king's accomplishments.

I pulled down these gates [Imgur-Ellil and Nemetti-Ellil] and laid their foundations at the water-table with asphalt and bricks and had them made of bricks with blue stone on which wonderful bulls and dragons were depicted. I covered their roofs by laying majestic cedars length-wise over them. I hung doors of cedar adorned with bronze at all the gateways and thus adorned them with luxurious splendor so that people might gaze on them in wonder.

I let the temple of Esiskursiskur be built firm like a mountain . . . of asphalt and fired bricks.

_____

(Source: "Dedicatory Inscription on the Ishtar Gate, Babylon," Ishtar Gate Inscription. Available online. URL: http://www.kchanson. com/ANCDOCS/meso/ishtarins.html. Accessed March 17, 2008.)

CONNECTIONS

The Babylonian Captivity

The Babylonian Captivity, when thousands of Jews from the kingdom of Judaea were forced into exile in Babylon, was a very important event in Jewish history. Nebuchadnezzar, the Babylonian king, twice laid siege to Jerusalem, in 589 and 588 B.C.E. The second siege lasted for 18 months. The king of Judaea finally surrendered in 586 B.C.E., mostly because his people were starving. The city was looted, and the palace and Temple were totally destroyed.

The Temple had been the central religious institution for the ancient Jews and its destruction was a heavy blow. In 538 B.C.E. Persian king Cyrus II, who had conquered Babylon, allowed the Jews to return to Judaea. They built a new Temple, which was completed around 530 B.C.E.

The Babylonian Captivity features prominently in the Old Testament of the Bible (or Tanakh). The prophets Ezekiel, Ezra, and Nehemiah are among the best sources for information about the period of exile.

Several well-known psalms are also based on this period, including Psalm 137. It says, "By the rivers of Babylon, there we sat, sat and wept, as we thought of Zion. There on the poplars we hung up our lyres, for our captors asked us there for songs . . . How can we sing a song of the Lord in a strange land?" (quoted in *The Jewish Study Bible*). (*Zion* is the Jewish homeland.)

If these words sound familiar, it is because they formed the basis for one of the most popular reggae songs of all time, *By the Rivers of Babylon*. This song was written and recorded by Brent Dowe and Trevor McNaughton of The Melodians in 1972. It became enormously popular, and over the years has been recorded by many others, including Bob Marley, Sinéad O'Connor, the Neville Brothers, and Sublime.

THE RISE OF THE PERSIANS

Beyond the Zagros Mountains in the east, a new civilization was emerging. These were the Persians, who lived in the land known today as Iran. In 550 B.C.E., a little more than 10 years after Nebuchadnezzar had died, Cyrus II (ca. 575–529 B.C.E.) became king in Anshan in western Persis. History credits Cyrus with being a skillful military leader and a talented ruler. He created an empire. Although he invaded many lands, he showed great respect for the people he conquered, and allowed them to keep their traditions and their religion.

Cyrus set up branches of his Persian government in each of the regions he ruled. These provinces were called satrapies, and the governors

We Come in Peace

Unlike the Assyrian kings before him, Cyrus did not seek to destroy the cities he conquered. When he entered Babylon in 539 B.C.E., he declared (as quoted in Persian Journal, http://www.iranian.ws/cyrus.htm), "I am Cyrus, the king of the world, great king, legitimate king (son of Cambyses) whose rule Bel and Nebo loved and whom they wanted as king to please their hearts. When I entered Babylon as a friend and established the seat of government in the place of the ruler under jubilation and rejoicing, Marduk, the great lord (induced) the magnanimous inhabitants of Babylon (to love me) and I daily endeavored to praise him. My numerous troops walked around in Babylon in peace, I did not allow anybody to terrorize (any of the people) of the country of Sumer and Akkad."

of these provinces were called satraps. Cyrus left the management of each province to the satraps. They ruled independently and had only a few responsibilities to Cyrus. They had to collect and send tax money to the king and provide men for Cyrus's army.

In 539 B.C.E., Cyrus led his army against Babylon. The Babylonian king, Nabonidus (r. ca. 555–539 B.C.E.), was not popular with his people. He chose to live in Taima, an oasis in northwest Arabia, and ignored his responsibilities in Babylon. According to legend, when Cyrus invaded the city, the Babylonians did not fight to keep him out. This quick and easy victory ended the power of Mesopotamia.

The overthrow of Nabonidus was actually accomplished by one of Cyrus's officers, Ugbaru [Gobryas], who became the governor after the conquest. Ugbaru claimed the land for Cyrus. He died a few months later, in 538 B.C.E.

Cyrus continued to move west and also conquered the Phoenicians. In 538 B.C.E., he captured Jerusalem and allowed the Jews who had been taken to Babylon to return to that city.

The days of the great empires of Mesopotamia had come to an end. The Mesopotamians no longer fought among themselves. For the first time in more than 20 centuries, the region had one strong central ruler who was able to govern its people.

Babylon was invaded again in the third century B.C.E. by the Greeks under Alexander the Great (356–323 B.C.E.). However, Babylon had lost its position as capital of the empire and most Babylonians decided to leave. By 141 B.C.E., Babylon was abandoned.

PART II

SOCIETY AND CULTURE

SUMERIAN CULTURE

BABYLONIAN CULTURE

ASSYRIAN CULTURE

CHAPTER 4

SUMERIAN CULTURE

SUMERIAN SOCIETY WAS ORGANIZED INTO THREE SOCIAL classes: *amelu, mushkinu,* and slaves. The *amelu* were the nobles, government officials, military officers, and priests. They were considered the upper class of Sumer. The class below the *amelu* were the *mushkinu.* This class was made up of merchants, farmers, brick makers, jewelers, leatherworkers, weavers, and other free workers.

The third and lowest social class was made up of slaves. Slavery was common in ancient Mesopotamia, but it was not permanent. Slaves were allowed to earn money, own property, and better themselves by learning a skill. Many slaves were able to buy their freedom.

Although most slaves were treated well, a slave could be branded or whipped. Efforts to run away from a master ended in severe punishment. Since the master depended on slaves' work, there was no advantage in treating a slave poorly. Most were well fed and healthy.

Slaves were sold in auctions in public marketplaces. They were also taken in war. Although having slaves was desirable, they were very expensive. The average price for a grown man was usually 20 shekels of silver. That same amount of silver could buy about 35 bushels of barley, which was enough grain to feed a small family for a year. Plus, a slave had to be fed, clothed, and housed. If a slave was ill, he also needed to see a doctor.

It was possible for free men and women to become slaves. People who owed debts could become slaves to pay off what they owed. Criminals could be forced into slavery as punishment for their crimes. A man could sell his children into slavery, and a man in debt could sell his

OPPOSITE
This early Sumerian stone sculpture shows an older couple sitting together with their arms around one another and holding hands.

The Slave's Contract
As with most aspects of Sumerian life, people sold into slavery had a contract listing their debt or term of slavery. The contract was written in clay to keep a record of it.

entire family to pay what he owed. The period during which the family worked as slaves was limited to three years.

Unlike slavery in the early years of the United States, Mesopotamian slaves had legal rights. One of those rights was the freedom to marry. If a slave married a free person, any children the pair had were free.

DAILY LIFE

Sumerians in cities lived in individual houses. The size of the house depended on the wealth of the owner. Kings lived in palaces with hundreds of rooms. Most members of the *mushkinu* class lived in small, one-story homes made of mud bricks. Those houses usually had five or six rooms. The houses usually shared common walls with neighbors and faced a small, open courtyard.

People of the *amelu* class might own a two-story home with twice as many rooms as the home of a *mushkinu* family. The home of a wealthy Sumerian was usually plastered and whitewashed both inside and out.

Typical rooms in Sumerian homes included sitting rooms, a bathroom, a kitchen, servants' quarters, and a private chapel. The walls were covered with reed mats and animal skins. Mats and skins might also be placed on the floor like rugs.

A clay model shows a Sumerian house divided into several rooms.

Mesopotamia was a dry, semi-desert area and had very little wood available for making furniture. So much of the furniture consisted of woven reeds set into a wooden frame. Common furniture items included low tables, high-backed chairs, and beds. Every household also had a variety of jars, pots, and plates made of clay, stone, copper, and bronze. Reed baskets and wooden chests held food, clothing, and other personal items.

Streets in the city were not paved and had no drainage to carry away rain and wastewater. On the rare occasions that it rained, the streets became quite muddy. The Sumerians did not have plumbing and sewers. They did not have garbage collection, either. People emptied pots of waste into the streets, along with any other garbage they had. When a layer of refuse formed in the street, it was covered with a thick layer of clay. Eventually, street levels became quite high and people used ladders to climb down to their homes.

THE SUMERIAN KITCHEN

The Sumerians ate a wide variety of foods. They used herbs and spices, such as salt, pepper, cumin, mustard, fennel, marjoram, thyme, mint, and rosemary. All of these herbs and spices can be found in most kitchens today. Most families had small pots of dried herbs available for both cooking and medicine.

Grains were commonly eaten in both bread and as hot cereal. Sumerians enjoyed more than 300 different varieties of bread. Most were flat loaves similar to the matzoh or pita bread that is still baked today. Most of the bread was made from barley, emmer (a type of

Who Did the Cooking?

Kings and people of the *amelu* class employed professional cooks. This was an honorable profession, since food fit for the king had to be well prepared. Most of these chefs were men. For the most part, women were not welcome in royal kitchens.

To make sure they were able to prepare special dishes the same way every time, cooks wrote down recipes. This one (from "Mesopotamian Menus") is for a meat pie. *Fowl* are domesticated birds and the *pluck* is the heart, liver, and lungs.

Carefully lay out the fowls on a platter; spread over them the chopped pieces of gizzard and pluck, as well as the small sêpêtu breads which have been baked in the oven; sprinkle the whole with sauce, cover with the prepared crust and send to the table.

In addition to recipes, the Sumerian habit of writing down nearly everything means historians can study grocery lists. Records of food delivered to the royal kitchens at Ur include suckling pigs, wood-pigeons, ducks, lambs, and geese.

An Unusual Snack

Art from ancient Mesopotamia shows servants carrying unusual treats to noble diners. Among these dishes were grasshoppers in pastry. A clay tablet also tells us that people ate meat-filled intestine casings—the world's first known sausages.

wheat), or flax, or combinations of grains. Sweet cakes were made from grain, honey, eggs, and spices.

Native palm trees provided dates, which could be eaten fresh, dried, or cooked in dishes. Since the Sumerians did not have sugar, dates, grapes, and honey provided sweetness in their diets. Although they did not eat salads, the Sumerians did eat lettuce, onions, and radishes. They grew beans, which they ate fresh or dried in the sun for later use.

Protein in the Sumerian diet came from fish, meat, and poultry. Since Sumerian cities were located beside rivers, fish were easily available. The Sumerians also ate farmed fish. Tablets tell of freshwater fish that had been raised in ponds as part of Mesopotamia's irrigation system. Meat consisted mainly of mutton (sheep), lamb, or goat. Whole cattle were slaughtered and roasted. Ducks, geese, and other birds were plucked, spiced, and roasted. People who were poor did not eat meat nearly as often as those who were wealthy.

Sumerians lived in a hot, dry climate, which was not suited to keeping meat or fish very long before it spoiled. They learned how to preserve those foods by curing them with salt and spices, drying them in the sun, or smoking the flesh over charcoal. The Sumerians also enjoyed what today is called a barbecue—they often cooked meat over open coals.

WOMEN, MARRIAGE, AND FAMILIES

The center of life for Sumerians was the family. In Sumer, a family meant a father, his wife, and their children. Father was the head of the household and had nearly all the power. He could divorce his wife for minor reasons. If his wife could not have children, he was entitled to take a second wife. However, if a woman took a second husband, she would have been whipped or stoned to death.

The father also had power over his children. He could sell his children into slavery. Under law, if a child struck a father in anger, the child could be killed. Striking a mother does not appear in the law, so there may not have been a penalty for such an act.

Sumerian marriages were often arranged by the couple's parents. When the parents chose a wife for a man, the engagement was announced. A marriage contract was written down and signed by both parties. The future husband provided a bride price, which was a payment for his new wife. This could be a gift to her family of jewels, furniture, grain, cattle, sheep, or any goods of value.

When a girl was born, she was considered her father's daughter until she got married. From the time of the engagement, the girl was considered a member of her husband's family. A woman was old enough for marriage by about age 15. Men married in their late teens or early 20s.

Although women had less power than men, they did have some legal rights. They could own property and run a business. They could learn to read and write, buy and sell property, borrow and lend money, and be priestesses in the temple. They could also be a witness at a trial if they saw a crime committed or knew that the accused person did not commit a crime. This freedom and power for women decreased sharply from the time the Sumerians were in power to the era of the Assyrians.

Sumerian myths and legends also featured women in positive roles. The mother-goddess Inanna was the creator of life, and the Sumerians believed she was also the goddess of fertility who helped ensure a good crop. Sumerians had a proverb that advised people, "Pay heed to the word of your mother as though it were the word of a god" (quoted on the Web site "Women in World History").

Girls were trained from childhood about how to manage a household. They learned how to buy and prepare foods for the two meals the family ate daily. Grinding grain into flour was important, since porridge and bread were eaten daily. Girls also had to learn how to make beer, wine, and grape juice. Many girls were taught to spin fiber into thread or yarn and to weave the thread into cloth.

Because women were involved in bearing and raising children, some women became midwives—women who deliver babies. While a sick Sumerian went to an herbal healer or doctor, a pregnant woman usually had her baby delivered by a midwife.

SUMERIAN CLOTHING

The clothing people wore depended on the materials they had available. Most ancient Sumerians, both men and women, wore sheepskin skirts with the skin facing inward and tufts of wool on the outside. The skirts wrapped around the body and were held in place by a large pin. Skirts covered the lower body to the knees. Nobles, officials, and military officers often wore ankle-length skirts. The upper body was bare or covered by a sheepskin cloak around the shoulders.

Beginning in about 2500 B.C.E., people changed from garments made of skin and raw wool to clothing made from wool fabric. Weavers

Women's Rights

The rights of Sumerian women may not sound very impressive, but it was not too long ago in the United States and Canada that women could not vote, own property, keep the money they earned, or serve on juries in trials. Women in Canada could not vote until 1919 and women in the United States could not vote until 1920. Five thousand years ago, women in Sumer had more legal rights than women in North America and Europe enjoyed 200 years ago.

were able to keep the look of wool tufts in the woven cloth, and this look remained popular. The tufts were either sewn on the cloth or woven into the fabric, and appear in most sculptures of people from this period.

Hairdos were important to the *amelu*. Wealthy men and women wore wigs with intricate hairdos. They also wore golden jewelry that often had gems set in the metal. Ornate pins held cloaks together. Lapis lazuli (a blue stone) and carnelian (an orange or orange-red stone) were popular and were used in necklaces, pendants, and bracelets. The *amelu* had professional hair stylists, and many decorated their hairdos with fancy headdresses.

Wealthy men and women wore wigs with intricate hairdos, fancy headdresses, and ornate jewelry. These are the hair ornaments, earrings, and jewelry of a rich woman.

CONNECTIONS

The War Congress

Long before the Greeks, the Romans, or the British had a legislature with two houses, the Sumerians had a congress much like the one in the United States. The upper house consisted of elders in the community and the lower house consisted of an assembly of men who would be part of an army in the event of war. The purpose of the two houses was to form a war congress—a body that discussed war and peace.

The elders usually voted for peace. The king generally would ignore their ruling in favor of war. Then, the lower house of warriors would vote for war, with the king's approval.

The first two-house congress met more than 5,000 years ago. While this may not have been a democracy like today's, it did have two groups that advised the king on issues that affected all the people. It is obvious, however, from the number of times that the Sumerians were at war that the king and his warriors had more power than the peace-loving elders.

Sumerians added a type of shawl or wrap to their general dress by about 2370 B.C.E. All people wore sandals on their feet.

THE SUMERIAN GODS

The Sumerians believed in many gods. An was the god of heaven, while Enlil was the god of the forces of nature and air. One god was responsible for the weather, another for the crops, and a third for family health and success. There was a god for cattle (Lahar) and one for grain (Ashnan). Some gods had multiple areas of power, such as Enki, the god of fertile earth, magic, and freshwater.

Goddesses played important roles as well. Nammu was the mother goddess and was said to have given birth to all the other gods. Inanna was goddess of love and war, while Ninshubur was the goddess of the morning star.

Most Sumerian gods had very human characteristics. Some bickered over who was in charge of what area. Some had tempers that, when angered, meant bad things happened to humans. Some gods brought peace or gave wisdom to the people. The gods and goddesses also controlled the daily events that affected each person's life.

Gods and goddesses were believed to marry. Kings of Sumer were considered to be gods or related to gods, and some were married to

Some Important Sumerian Gods

GOD*	GODDESS*	AREA OF POWER
	Inanna (Ishtar)	Love
Ninurta	Inanna (Ishtar)	War
Nergal	Ereshkigal	Underworld
An (Anu) (father of the gods)	Nammu (mother goddess)	Heaven
Enlil (Ellil)	Ninlil	Earth, forces of nature
	Zarima and Zurma (twins)	Clouds
Enki (Ea)	Ki	Fertile earth, magic, water
Nanna (Sin)		Moon
Utu (Shamash)		Sun
Ishkur (Adad)		Rain

*If a deity was worshipped by both the Sumerians (Sumerian name) and the Babylonians and Assyrians (Akkadian name) the Sumerian name is given first, followed by the Akkadian name in parentheses.

goddesses. For example, Uruk's King Tammuz was the husband of the goddess Inanna.

The forces of nature—rain, thunder and lightning, water, and the earth—had individual gods. Together, these gods were called the Nephilim, which means "those who from Heaven to Earth came down" in Hebrew. Flooding, for example, was considered to be a punishment created by an underwater demon god who ruled from under the Gulf of Persia.

The Sumerians believed in an afterlife. When people died, they went to an underworld beneath the surface of the earth. This was a harsh place from which the people could not escape.

Most people were buried in crypts (rooms, usually underground, that are used for burying bodies) under the floors of their homes. The average body of a *mushkinu* was buried with some household possessions. The *amelu* were buried with jewelry, fine clothing, golden cups, and a large number of servants.

There were cemeteries, but they were not as commonly used as burial beneath the family home. Burial in a cemetery was expensive. The dead person's family was expected to pay cemetery officials with bread, barley, wine, and dates. This was a major expense for a family.

THE ROLE OF THE TEMPLE

The Sumerians believed the gods created human beings to serve them. To provide that service, every city had at least one central temple. The central temple usually had smaller areas dedicated to individual gods. With the large number of gods that needed to be worshipped, Sumerian temples were busy places.

If the people served the gods, the gods, in turn, also served the people. They kept cities safe, their people fed, and their workers prosperous. Temples owned large tracts of land, and the temple priests or priestesses

Inanna in the Underworld

To the Sumerians, Inanna was the most important goddess. She was the goddess of love, fertility, and war. She was also the daughter of An and Nammu, the father and mother of the gods.

Inanna, also called Ishtar, appeared in various myths and legends. In one story, Inanna claimed to rule the underworld and all the people there. This did not suit the goddess Ereshkigal, Inanna's sister, who actually ruled the underworld. Ereshkigal was so angry that she sentenced Inanna to death.

Inanna's death brought great tragedy to the land. All plants died with her; nothing would grow. But since gods never really die, all this meant was that Inanna was trapped in the underworld.

Inanna escaped the underworld with the help of the god Enki. Enki said Inanna could be reborn if another person would take her place in the underworld. She chose her husband Tammuz. From that time, Tammuz existed in the underworld for half of every year. This myth helps explain the seasonal cycle of plant life. The plants thrive for the half-year Inanna is free from the underworld and die when she must return.

arranged rituals (ceremonies carried out according to religious laws and customs), sacrifices, and the work that supported the temple.

A temple needed someone to run the business that occurred within it. This could be either a man or a woman. The temple manager arranged the planting and harvesting of crops on temple property, herding the sheep or goats, distributing the food, and the other businesses that supported temple life.

Some temples started out as a small shrine to a specific god. But as a city grew, its temples grew. A large, wealthy temple was the sign of a large, wealthy city. A wealthy temple needed treasure rooms, offices, a brewery, a pottery, storehouses for grain and other food, and an arsenal to store weapons. Maintaining the temple required many employees, some of whom lived on the temple grounds. The most important were the head priest or priestess and the supporting priests and priestesses. There were also scribes, accountants, musicians, artists, cooks, cleaners, and servants. And there were hundreds of farmers, shepherds, and herdsmen to tend the land and cattle belonging to the temple.

In the case of the temple of the goddess Bau in Lagash, the manager was, at one time, Queen Shagshag (r. ca. 2350 B.C.E.). She was also the chief priestess. Managing the temple was no small undertaking, because it had more than 1,000 workers. Temple workers included 150 slave women who brewed beer, ground grain, spun and wove wool, and worked in the kitchens. The temple also had six women in charge of feeding the pigs, 15 cooks to feed the 1,000 employees, and a brewery with 46 workers. The queen had personal servants to mind her children and attend her, plus a personal hairdresser. There was also a singer and a handful of musicians to provide entertainment.

Women were responsible for caring for their families, and this included the responsibility to pray in the temple. Women from the *amelu* class had statues made to represent them at the temple. The statue was posed to look like a woman praying. The statue would be left at the temple in what appeared to be constant prayer while the woman went about her daily business.

SUMERIAN ENTERTAINMENT

Sumerians enjoyed music. Singers and musicians played a major role in religious festivals, as well. Common instruments included various types of drums and stringed instruments. Lyres (stringed instruments, similar to harps) and harps were common, and the remnants of those instruments have been found in the ruins of Ur among other cities. Lyres found in

Sumerian palace ruins were made of wood with ornaments of gold and lapis lazuli.

Drums were common in both temples and palaces, and they came in many sizes and shapes. There was a type of hand drum that was much like a tambourine. The larger drums were shaped like hourglasses or were bowl-shaped kettledrums. Along with the drums, Sumerians played several types of cymbals and bells. They also enjoyed horns, pipes, and whistles. The largest horns were much like today's trumpets. They were used on the battlefield to rally the troops to battle.

This game board and playing pieces were found in the Royal Cemetery of Ur. The game looks similar to the modern game of backgammon.

Royal courts had a wide variety of entertainers. Jugglers delighted their audiences. Singers and dancers were common dinnertime entertainment. The *amelu* also enjoyed watching athletes compete in wrestling or military-style games.

The Sumerians played a number of games. A game board from the Royal Cemetery of Ur (ca. 26th century B.C.E.) appears to be a combination of markers and squares. The markers are round and come in two colors—one for each player. The game looks like a simple variety of the modern game of backgammon. Games of chance included one in which differently shaped and colored stones were placed in a jar. Bets were made on which would tumble out first, and the luck of the winners was left in the hands of the gods.

Girls played with dolls, and had dollhouses and tiny furniture to include in their games. Boys had miniature carts and war figures. Boys also had bows and arrows, spears, and other weapons of war with which they played soldier. Boys played with toy warships and chariots, too. Children in general enjoyed playing with spinning tops, hoops, and balls. There was a game much like jump rope, called the game of Ishtar.

LITERATURE

Literature played an important role in the daily lives of Sumerians. Many people in Sumer could read, and those who could not would listen to stories and tales. Most nobles, merchants, and military officers learned to read in school. Few farmers, slaves, or workers could read. Scribes were hired to write official documents and to read documents and letters for those who could not read. They also recorded official events and announcements made by kings and other nobles.

The Sumerian Creation Story

Like many cultures, the Sumerians had a creation story that explained the arrival of humans on earth. They believed that at one time water covered all the earth. This earliest time was called chaos—a condition of complete confusion or disorder. Tiamat, a huge dragon, ruled over the chaos. The gods tried to make order from chaos, and this angered the dragon Tiamat. Tiamat created an army of dragons to attack the gods.

The god of the air, Enlil, called the winds to help him defeat the dragons. Tiamat came forward with her mouth wide open. Enlil forced the winds inside her, making Tiamat puff up so fat that she could not move. Enlil cut her body open and formed the earth from one half of Tiamat's huge body. He used the other half of Tiamat to form the sky.

To make human beings, the gods cut off the head of Tiamat's husband. They mixed his blood with the clay of the earth and created human beings.

Epic poems raised ordinary kings to the level of gods. They sang of the heroism, daring, and cunning of humans, and made those humans sound larger than life. Epic poems often carried a moral, delivered advice, or dealt with problems people faced in daily life. The best known of the Mesopotamian epic poems is *The Epic of Gilgamesh*. Gilgamesh was a Sumerian ruler honored for his wisdom and understanding.

Hymns and prayers were another form of literature. So were proverbs. These are short sayings that give advice to the people. Because they are so short, they are easy to remember. For those who could not read, they were a form a "literature" that they could pass on through their family.

For many years, historians believed that the Bible's book of Proverbs was the first collected group of sayings. Then historians found similar proverbs in Egyptian literature that were even older. However, the archaeological dig at Nippur uncovered many proverbs and sayings that were older still. This led historians to believe that the Sumerians may have developed the first proverbs and sayings in the world.

One well-known Sumerian proverb (quoted in Samuel Noah Kramer's *History Begins at Sumer*) deals with the problems of the poor:

The poor man is better dead than alive;
If he has bread, he has no salt,
If he has salt, he has no bread,
If he has meat, he has no lamb,
If he has lamb, he has no meat.

Another one (also quoted by Kramer) gives advice about what will be of value to a man.

The desert canteen is a man's life,
The shoe is a man's eye,
The wife is a man's future,
The son is a man's refuge,

IN THEIR OWN WORDS

The Sumerian Flood Story

History records many legends of floods that washed away the entire world. One such flood appears in Sumerian history in about 2300 B.C.E. The story is much like the story of Noah in the Bible. According to the tale, the gods created humans and were disappointed in their creation. So they sent a flood to destroy all traces of human beings on earth.

The main players in the story are Utu, the sun god, and Ziusudra, a Sumerian king. A six-day rainstorm forced floodwaters to rush through the Euphrates River. The river rose 15 cubits (a cubit is an ancient measure of length, equal to about the length of a forearm), overflowed its banks, and flooded the city-states of Sumer. When the banks overflowed, Ziusudra boarded a river barge. When the flooding stopped, Ziusudra offered a sacrifice on an altar at the top of a nearby hill. The flood came to an end and human beings gained another chance from the gods.

Here is an excerpt from the Sumerian legend.

[A] flood will sweep over the cult-centers;
To destroy the seed of mankind . . .
Is the decision, the word of the assembly
of the gods.
By the word commanded by Anu and Enlil . . .
Its kingship, its rule will be put to an end.. . .
All the windstorms, exceedingly powerful,
Attacked as one,
At the same time, the flood sweeps over the cult-centers.
After, for seven days and seven nights,
The flood had swept over the land,
And the huge boat had been tossed
About by the windstorms on the great waters,
Utu came forth, who sheds light on heaven and earth,
Ziusudra opened a window of the huge boat,
The hero Utu brought his rays into the giant boat.
Ziusudra, the king,
Prostrated himself before Utu.

(Source: "The Flood," excerpted from S. Dalley, *Myths from Mesopotamia.* Available online. URL: http://web.archive. org/web/19990221091328/http://puffin. creighton.edu/theo/simkins/tx/Flood.html. Accessed March 21, 2008.)

The daughter is a man's salvation,
The daughter-in-law is a man's devil.

In other words, carrying water will save a man's life in the desert. His future depends on having a wife, because she will provide him with children. Sons and daughters have great value, but when the son marries, there will be problems.

SUMERIAN SCHOOLS

Sumerian schools were not for everyone. Only the *amelu* sent their children to school. Although both girls and boys could attend school, most students were boys. Generally, girls were destined for marriage and motherhood, and many fathers saw no reason to pay the high fees charged by scribes to educate their daughters.

Classes were held in buildings called tablet houses, and the teachers were called "fathers of the tablet houses." This was where young people learned to read and write. Classes ran from sunup to sundown—a long day.

Students learned cuneiform, which was not easy to write. Cuneiform was made up of combinations of wedges and lines, which were formed in groups. There were more than 600 types of wedges and lines, which could be combined into thousands of groups. Sumerian students learned writing by copying their teachers. Each student got a tablet of wet clay and a triangular reed, called a stylus. The teacher wrote on the left side of the tablet and the student wrote on the right side. Erasing was easy: Just smooth out the clay and start again.

Students also learned mathematics. The Sumerians used two number systems. The first was a base-10 or decimal system. That is the same kind of number system used today. The second system was based on the number 60—the result of multiplying 10 times 6. The advantage of the number 60 is that it can be divided by 2, 3, 4, 5, 6, 10, 12, 15, 20, and 30.

SUMERIAN INVENTIONS AND INNOVATIONS

Cuneiform was probably the most important Sumerian invention. Writing was a form of communication used every day. Although the written language was difficult and took years to learn, writing was the foundation for major advances in business, government, and social contracts.

IN THEIR OWN WORDS

Examinations for a Student Scribe

Students in Sumerian schools had end-of-year examinations. One tablet found by archaeologists recorded the tests given by a scribe to his son. Here is the list of topics covered in the exam:

1. The element of the scribal craft is the simple wedge; it has six teeth [directions in which it could be written]. . . . Do you know its name?
2. Secret meanings of Sumerian words. . . . .
3. Translation from Sumerian to Akkadian and the reverse.
4. Three Sumerian synonyms for each Akkadian word.
5. Sumerian grammatical terminology.
6. Sumerian conjugation of verbs.
7. Various types of calligraphy and technical writing.
8. Writing Sumerian phonetically.
9. To understand the technical language of all classes of priests and other professions, such as silversmiths, jewelers, herdsmen, and scribes.
10. How to write, make an envelope, and seal a document.
11. All kinds of songs and how to conduct a choir.
12. Mathematics, division of fields, and allotting of rations.
13. Various musical instruments.

It should be noted that the student failed and blamed his teacher—his father—for his lack of success.

(Source: Nemet-Nejat, Karen Rhea. *Daily Life in Ancient Mesopotamia.* Westport, Conn.: Greenwood Press, 1998.)

Keeping records required the Sumerians to develop a number system and methods of using those numbers. Government records listed the number of sheep in a flock, people in a city, and baskets of grain in a harvest. The value of products needed to be added up. Taxes had to be subtracted from the entire amount. The taxes were multiplied by the number of people in a community to determine the wealth of a city-state. Foodstuffs were divided among the people. The Sumerians found uses for mathematics that had never occurred before.

One major use of mathematics was in developing the calendar. The Sumerian solar year was divided into two seasons. The summer was the time of barley harvests. Winter was the equivalent of modern-day fall and winter.

This calendar was not sufficient for regular use, for many reasons. The calendar changed from one city to the next. A month name in Uruk was most likely different from the same month name in

The Royal Cemetery at Ur

Ur was an ancient Sumerian city, located in present-day Iraq. In the 1920s, British archaeologist Charles Leonard Woolley (1880–1960) was the person in charge of a joint venture between the British Museum and the University of Pennsylvania to excavate the ancient city. In the course of his work, he found a royal cemetery that turned out to be the most spectacular of any found in the ancient Near East.

The burials were made some time around 2500 B.C.E., and they remained undisturbed until Woolley and his team found them. Inside these tombs was a treasure trove of ancient artifacts. There were large paintings of ancient Sumerian culture at its highest point, along with gold and silver jewelry, cups, and other furnishings.

Some of the tombs could be identified as belonging to specific people, such as the tomb of Queen Puabi, who lived some time between 2600 B.C.E. and 2500 B.C.E. Others have been given general names according to the artifacts found in the graves. The Great Death Pit, for example, contained the remains of more than 74 servants who died so that they could serve their master in the afterlife.

One of the most beautiful objects found in the cemetery was the Standard of Ur. This may have been the sounding box for a type of stringed instrument. The sides are lapis lazuli inlaid with cut shells. Figures line up in three rows, and include humans and animals. It looks as if the people are preparing for a banquet. There are people from all walks of life represented on this panel: kings, servants, soldiers, farmers, weavers, and dozens of other professions.

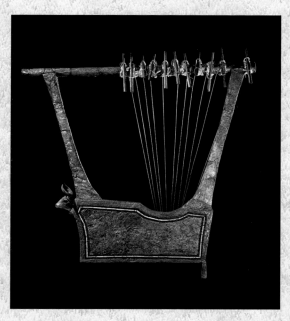

This wooden lyre covered with silver was found in the Royal Cemetery of Ur. On the left side is a bull's head.

Lagash. Within the Sumerian city of Babylon, one month might have several names. Most month names were chosen according to the religious festivals taking place that month. Within a city, brick makers might have one favorite god while barley farmers followed another. For each group, the month name they used would be different.

CONNECTIONS

Clocks and Circles

Why does an hour have 60 minutes and a minute have 60 seconds? Why does a circle have 360 degrees? This interest in the number 60 comes from the Sumerians. The Sumerians divided time by units relating to the numbers 6 and 60. They divided circles into 360 degrees (360 is 60 times 6). They also gathered items by the dozen (12 is 2 times 6, and there are 5 dozen in 60).

Records required dating, which meant that the Sumerians needed a calendar that was the same for everyone. They also needed to count the years, which they did in cycles of 60 years. In that way, a business agreement could be dated as written on a certain day in a certain year, and everyone would know what was meant.

The earliest calendar was connected to when crops were planted or harvested, or other financial events. This was not an accurate way to mark time. So the Sumerians devised a more accurate calendar by 2400 B.C.E. The new calendar had 30 days in each of 12 months, or 360 days per year. Every third year, the Sumerians had a short "catch-up" month to make up for there being five too few days in a year. This "catch-up" month is equivalent to the modern leap year.

Farming communities were also sites of major innovations that can be traced to Sumerian invention. The early Sumerians saw that the land they farmed was much too dry. To bring water to the crops, they developed a system of canals and ditches to carry the water. This enabled farmers to produce more crops. Increased food crops fed an increasing number of people. Out of these farm communities emerged the world's first cities—places such as Eridu and Uruk.

Canals and irrigation also led to two other remarkable ideas: shade-tree gardens and fish farms. The first shade-tree garden must have been a welcome oasis (fertile land in the desert where there are trees and water) from the dry, desert climate of Mesopotamia. One advantage of having water carried through canals is that it becomes a simple matter to fill pools of water. The Sumerians farmed fish in the pools, and they were the first culture to do so.

CHAPTER 5

BABYLONIAN CULTURE

BABYLON WAS THE CAPITAL OF THE BABYLONIAN EMPIRE. The Euphrates River flowed through the center of the city and divided it into two parts. It was also a religious and trade center. The earliest mention of the city's existence appears in tablets that date from the reign of Sargon I of Akkad. During the reign of Hammurabi, it became a capital city.

During the reign of King Nebuchadnezzar II, the city developed into an architectural wonder. The Hanging Gardens of Babylon and the Tower of Babel are among Nebuchadnezzar's major building projects.

Three layers of walls surrounded and protected the city. The inner walls measured 20 feet deep. The third layer of walls was also protected by a moat. People entered through elaborately decorated gates. The Ishtar Gate was the most spectacular, decorated with figures of bulls and dragons. Another entrance called the Processional Way was used for formal entrances. Within the city, people prayed at temples dedicated to Marduk, Ishtar, Ninurta, and other popular Babylonian gods.

Surrounding every city-state, including Babylon, was a large area for farming and raising livestock. Herds grazed in the grasslands west of the Euphrates River. The government kept track of the great herds of sheep, goats, and cattle, because most of those animals belonged to either the king or the local temple.

Men were hired by the animals' owners to work as herdsmen or shepherds, and they watched over many flocks. One shepherd might be responsible for some sheep belonging to the king, some to the temple, and others to a local noble. Such herdsmen and shepherds were paid for their work in the form of silver, grain or other food, oil, wine, or other goods.

OPPOSITE
The Ishtar Gate, decorated with figures of bulls and dragons, was the most spectacular way to enter the city of Babylon.

CONNECTIONS

The Tower of Babel

The story of the Tower of Babel is in the book of Genesis in the Bible. According to the story, all the humans on earth originally spoke the same language. They settled in what the Bible calls the land of Shinar—Mesopotamia. There they decided to build a city, and in that city they started building a huge ziggurat.

Genesis, chapter 10, verse 4 says, "And they said, 'Come, let us build us a city, and a tower with its top in the sky, to make a name for ourselves, else we shall be scattered all over the world'" (quoted in *The Jewish Study Bible*). But God was angry at the people for thinking they could reach to the sky and for having the pride to think that works made by humans would be considered more lasting and famous than works made by God. So he caused them all to speak different languages, and because they could not understand one another, they had to stop building the tower.

In verse 9 it says, "That is why it was called Babel, because there the Lord confounded the speech of the whole earth; and from there the Lord scattered them over the face of the whole earth." The name *Babel* is a play on the Hebrew word *balal*, which means confound or confuse.

Today, *babble* means to talk fast and in a foolish way, or the sound of a lot of people talking in a way that is hard to understand. The word comes from this Bible story. So does the name of the city of Babylon.

But was there really a Tower of Babel? Archaeologists studying the ruins of ancient Babylon think there was. They know the Mesopotamians built ziggurats to honor their gods. When Babylon was the most influential city in Mesopotamia, its ziggurat honoring the god Marduk was the tallest tower in the region. Archaeologists examining the remains of the city have found what appears to be the foundation of this tower. Its square base was 300 feet on each side and it was about 295 feet high.

The tower was rebuilt several times, and reached its most magnificent heights under King Nebuchadnezzar II. Inscriptions made by the king say the tower was made of baked bricks covered with brilliant blue enamel, and its terraces may have been planted with gardens.

BABYLONIAN SOCIETY

Just like the Sumerians, the Babylonians had three social classes. The upper class was *awilum*, and included all the property owners and wealthy people. At the very top were the king, queen, princes and princesses, and other nobles. Priests and priestesses of the temples were also among the *awilum*, as were military leaders.

Being a member of this class was basically a matter of birth, but rising into the *awilum* was possible. A craftsman who created wonderful products could sell them, earn a lot of money, and become wealthy. A soldier who was exceptionally brave and successful might be promoted and become a captain or general.

The *awilum* were expected to pay taxes on their wealth and to participate in the military. When a gentleman of the *awilum* died, his property and riches were passed on to his sons. Daughters did not receive part of the wealth, because they were expected to marry and join their husband's family. It was important to keep riches within the family, and giving wealth to a daughter meant giving the wealth to another family.

The middle class was called the *mushkenum*. The Babylonian *mushkenum* consisted of craftsmen, artisans, merchants, farmers, and other skilled workers.

SLAVERY IN BABYLONIA

The lowest class was the slaves, called *wardum*. Slavery was an established practice throughout Mesopotamia. Slaves could belong to the state (that is, the king), to a temple, or to a private owner. A person became a slave in several ways. When the military invaded a land, the people of the defeated land often became slaves. They were forced to travel from their homelands to the cities of their captors. Many were sold in the market. Other people became slaves because they were guilty of crimes or owed money.

State slaves were used to do whatever work the king wanted done. They built palaces, served the *awilum*, dug ditches, paved roads, and made bricks. They lived in state housing. State slaves might even be used in the military. Their names, ages, and homelands were recorded on clay tablets and kept by state officials.

Temple slaves were treated slightly differently. During a drought or in the event of a crop failure, parents might give their children to the temple to be slaves. While this seems cruel, it saved many children's lives. The temple owned land and harvested crops. It also stored a great deal of food for later use, so children given to the temple might well have been saved from starving to death. Life in the temple was a life of safety. Slaves always had clothes, fires in the winter, and food and drink. Many temple slaves had better lives than many free workers in the city.

Privately owned slaves could be forced to work at any job. For example, an innkeeper might purchase a slave. That slave might be told to clean, wash linens or clothing, wait on tables, cook, or make beer. A farm slave might work the fields beside his or her owner. A female slave might tend children in a home, cook, or clean. A slave who had been trained to read and write might be expected to work as a scribe. Slaves worked side by side with free workers. If a nobleman needed to build a canal and irrigation ditches on the land he owned, he hired a number of workers and also used slaves.

The average price of a slave in Babylonian times was about 20 shekels of silver. A highly skilled slave, such as a scribe or a goldsmith, might sell for more. Some went for as much as 30 shekels of silver—the equivalent of 30 bushels of barley or a few sheep or goats.

The law required that slaves be treated decently. They were protected by law from injury. They could earn wages, own property, and, if they were lucky, buy their freedom. A skilled slave, such as a weaver or a tanner (a person who works with leather), could succeed in a city where such skills were needed. Such a slave could earn money and eventually buy his freedom.

In some situations, slaves had better lives than free workers. For example, if a slave was injured, the law said it was his owner's responsibility to pay for a doctor and to continue to feed and house the slave when he could not work. A free worker, on the other hand, had to pay for the doctor himself and had no one to care for him while he could not work.

However, slaves could not run away or fail to do their work. They were not free to choose where they lived or whom they worked with. A runaway slave might be whipped or branded, but few were killed. There was no profit in killing such a valuable possession. It was also against the law to steal someone else's slave. If a person was caught stealing a slave, the punishment could be as little as a steep fine or as serious as loss of a limb or one's life.

CONNECTIONS

Contracts

The Sumerians, Babylonians, and Assyrians were great believers in the value of a business contract. Of the thousands of documents found from those ancient times, most are business or legal contracts. Most major events in a person's life were part of a contract. Contracts recorded sales of goods or property, deeds of ownership, gifts, marriages, adoptions, and debts. If a person broke a contract, the court would make them pay a fine worth from three to 30 times the value of the contract.

The child of a slave was also a slave. It was against the law to sell the children of slaves away from their parents. Slave children were sometimes adopted by their owners. As adopted children, they were expected to care for their parents as the parents got older. When their adopted parents died, the slave children became free. They also inherited property from their adopted parents.

MARRIAGE AND FAMILY

The center of Babylonian life was the family. The father was the head of the family, and what father said was the law. Wives and children were expected to obey their fathers, and later their husbands, in all things. Although women and children had some legal rights, the majority of rights belonged to the husbands.

When the father died, his oldest unmarried son became the head of the family. The son had all the same rights regarding the remaining children as his father had. He, too, could sell his brothers and sisters into slavery. He could arrange marriages for his younger siblings. If all the children were young, sometimes the mother would be given the legal right to act as a father would.

Most Babylonians expected to get married when they reached adulthood. It was important to have children because children supported their elderly parents. Both men and women generally married in their mid to late teens.

Marriage was a business deal between two fathers. The arrangements were made and a contract was drawn up regarding the deal. The father of the bride set a price for his daughter that had to be paid by the bridegroom. A common bride price was one shekel or mina, and the price depended on the groom's wealth. The bride went into marriage with a dowry—money or gifts from her family. The dowry might be silver, gold, or gems from an *awilum* family, or a basket of grain or a sheep from a *mushkenum* family.

Very little is known about the marriage ceremony except that it was probably brief. The husband and wife exchanged vows, and they were married. The vows may have been something like, "I will fill your lap with silver and gold: You are my wife; I am your husband" (quoted in Karen Nemet-Nejat's *Daily Life in Ancient Mesopotamia*). Once married, the woman belonged to her husband's family.

If the marriage did not go smoothly, divorce was quick and easy. The husband said, "You are not my wife." The wife said, "You are not my husband." The marriage was at an end. Whatever dowry the wife

Father's Legal Advantage

Under the laws published by Hammurabi, a son who hit his father would have his hand cut off. A husband who wanted to divorce his wife could do so fairly easily. And if the wife did not give birth to sons, the husband could take a second wife. If the father failed to support his family and went into debt, he could sell his children and wife into slavery to pay that debt. Although he had the right to buy them back once the debt was paid, he was not required to do so.

brought to the marriage had to be returned to the wife if the marriage was dissolved. If the husband had spent the dowry and could not return it, divorce was not possible. In many cases, this probably was a major reason not to get divorced.

THE ROLE OF WOMEN

Babylonian women were allowed to own property and run businesses. Most businesses owned by women probably developed from their jobs in the home. A woman who made excellent bread might sell her bread in a stall in the market. Weaving, brewing beer, and sewing were other common jobs for women outside the home.

However, women were not limited to these jobs. Some women became scribes, which was a highly prized skill. *Awilum* women could become priestesses in the temple and have a wide array of women servants, clerks, and entertainers. Most priestesses were not allowed to marry, but those who could marry were not supposed to have children.

Women could also be doctors, fortunetellers, artists, and jewelry makers. However, it was more likely that a woman would be a fortuneteller than a doctor because men also worked as doctors and a woman doctor was in direct competition with a man. This was not true of fortunetellers, who were mostly women.

A woman's main role in life was to produce children. Generally, only one of every two children born to a family survived to adulthood. In hard times, such as drought, famine, or epidemics (widespread disease), the death rate for children increased. One reason some children died was that their mothers could not produce enough milk to feed them. *Awilum* mothers could hire a wet nurse—a woman who would breastfeed a child as a job.

This is part of a Babylonian sculpture of a woman wearing many necklaces.

Because a man's family name was carried by his sons, most parents wished for sons more than for daughters. Several sons guaranteed parents a solid future. Soon after a child was born, it was named. Sons carried the father's personal name but would also have other names, including the name of an ancestor. For example, a son might be named Iddin-Marduk, son of Iquisha, descendant of Nur-sin. Children sometimes got new names when they became adults.

Parents who did not have children of their own often adopted children. The adopted children had the same legal rights as naturally born children. Adopted sons could inherit property from their fathers. Adopted daughters were provided with dowries when they married.

CONNECTIONS

Family Names

Everyone today has a family name and a given name. The given name is the one they got from their parents. The family name is the name that is passed on through the generations.

It was during the time of the Babylonians that people started using family names. Free men were known by their father's name, so having sons and grandsons became important to carry on the family name. Slaves did not have last names.

Family names sometimes came from the father's profession. Many people who had family names were scribes. However, there were also families called goldsmith, carpenter, or silversmith.

Today, many family names originally came from the relationship between father and son, such as Johnson, Wilson, Davison, Jackson, Thompson, and Anderson. Others come from professions, such as Smith, Miller, Taylor, Fisher, Farmer, Baker, Turner, and Archer.

Adoption was not limited to infants. Many families adopted children and teens. The adoptive parents paid the child's family for the right to adopt, and also paid for the costs of raising the child. Even adults could be adopted. If elderly parents lost all their children—which might happen through disease or war—they could adopt adults. This would be particularly handy if the parents needed care. Adult children could take care of their new parents as they aged. In turn, the adopted children inherited their new parents' property.

THE FAMILY AT HOME

The Babylonian family lived together in a house. The average house included several small rooms, although wealthier families had larger homes. People slept in bedrooms, washed in washrooms, and ate

CONNECTIONS

Scrubbing with Soap

It was the Babylonians who discovered how to make soap. This may well have been an accident. A man or woman may have splashed melted animal fat on ashes from the fire, and the mess foamed. A slave who had to clean cooking pans may have mixed ash into the fat coating such a pan and found that the fatty ash made cleaning pans easier. This process of mixing fat and ash was refined, and eventually, anyone who made quality soaps earned a good living.

The common formula for soap was written down on a clay tablet. The earliest written soap formula consisted of cassia oil, alkali (from ashes), and water. It was written in 2200 B.C.E.

Wealthy Babylonians would first rub their bodies with a form of soap made from ashes and animal fat. Once covered with suds, servants poured jars of water over them to rinse off the soap.

at tables in the main living room.

The family ate once in the morning and once in the early evening. Wealthier families had more variety and more meat in their diets than poor families—fresh meat was expensive. The poorer the family, the more grain products they ate, because grain was cheap and easy to obtain. Most people ground their own grain into flour. As with the Sumerians, bread was made from barley, wheat, and other grains and was eaten at most meals. Rich or poor, the family gathered at the table and ate together.

Most Babylonians rose with the sun and went to bed at sunset. They slept in beds made of wooden frames topped with mattresses stuffed with wool, goat hair, or palm leaves. The *mushkenum* slept on mats made of reeds or mattresses filled with straw. The *awilum* had fine linen sheets and woolen blankets on their beds.

Food was cooked over hot coals or baked in clay ovens. An average family would have pottery jars and baskets for storage. *Awilum* might also have wooden chests for storing clothing, spices, or other goods. A well-stocked kitchen would have pots for cooking, dishes for serving, and knives and forks for eating. Cooks used salt, herbs, and other spices to flavor the food.

For most people, life was a matter of surviving. They rose each day, ate, worked, ate, and went to sleep each night. The majority of the people worked to get food, shelter, and clothing. They had few luxuries and very little entertainment. Only the wealthy *awilum* could afford fine clothes, plenty of food, and a comfortable lifestyle.

Palaces and the homes of the *awilum* had separate washrooms for bathing. Washing was done with either water or scented oil. Water had to be carried into these washrooms, so Babylonians did not usually bathe in tubs.

Bathrooms of the wealthy were large, spacious areas, about 15 feet by 15 feet. The lower walls were made from glazed bricks. The floor was also brick, but a layer of bitumen (an oily substance similar to tar) was added to make the floor waterproof. The Babylonians did not have sewers like the ones that carry water from tubs, toilets, and basins today. To get rid of excess water, they Babylonians slanted the floor of the bathroom. The water ran to the lower area, where a brick drain allowed the excess water to pass through into the soil below.

BUSINESS IN BABYLONIA

Daily, goods from far and wide arrived in the Babylonian marketplace. Caravans crossed the desert carrying spices, stone, copper, and gold. Teak (a type of hard wood) from India and cotton from Egypt made its way into Babylonia. From the north, traders brought marble, iron, and precious metals. The Babylonians set up market stalls to sell pottery, leather goods, jewelry, cloth, and a range of foods.

Most goods were sold by barter—a system of trading goods for other goods of equal value. A merchant traded a certain weight of peppercorns, for example, for another amount of wheat or barley. The grain

CONNECTIONS

Weights and Currency

Many things today are sold by weight, including most of the food items in the supermarket. U.S. law requires that weights be clearly marked and accurate. Scales in the meat, deli, or produce sections of supermarkets are checked by government officials to make sure that they are correct. This is not a new idea.

The Mesopotamians also used standardized weights when conducting business. Just as it is today, if the weights were not accurate, the shopkeeper paid a large fine. Most weights were carved from stone, but some merchants used fancier weights made of metal. A common shape for weights was that of a duck with its head tucked under its wing.

Weights were based on specific standards. The smallest weight was a barleycorn, equal to the weight of one grain of barley. Heavier weights included shekels, minas, and talents or loads. A shekel equaled 180 barleycorns. There were 60 shekels to a mina and 60 minas to a talent. Eventually, shekels and talents evolved into terms for money. The ancient Greeks and Romans had a unit of silver known as a talent. Today, Israel's currency is the sheqel (plural: *sheqalim*).

seller kept a portion of the pepper and traded the rest for a bolt of cloth or a knife or a stack of bricks with which to repair his house.

In the early days of Sumer, all trade was made in the form of goods. By the end of the Babylonian era, people had begun using metal to represent wealth or goods. Silver bars were made that were equal to specific weights. For example, a silver bar worth a shekel weighed slightly more than half an ounce (about 15 grams). Although this was much like money, the bars were not coins. The Babylonians simply found using these metal bars much easier than trading three goats for a cow.

The use of this early form of money led to the rise of a new profession—moneylenders. Money was loaned out to borrowers on the condition that it was paid back within a certain time, along with interest. Workers could borrow money against the value of their labor, farmers against their crops. If people could not pay their debts, they could be forced to work as slaves to pay what they owed.

The Babylonians recognized the importance of skilled craftsmanship. This is a stone model of a chariot.

OCCUPATIONS

Most Babylonians worked in some form of agriculture. The most important crops were various types of grain. Everyone in a city was affected by the success or failure of a grain crop. If the crop failed for any reason, the people went hungry. Kings and priests may have eaten meat, but everyone ate grain. Because grain was so important, the Babylonians built a system of irrigation trenches to water their fields.

The majority of land was farmed for the king or the local temple, but there were also tenant farmers who rented the land of others and paid their rent from the harvest. The agricultural year began in the early autumn when the landowner and tenant agreed on a contract. Rent for land use equaled about one-third of the year's crop. The harvest became a gift to the temples, and it was through the temples that grain was distributed to the local people.

The economy supported many other occupations, as well. Skilled traders and crafts-men earned their livings in the cities. A large city such as Babylon would have car-penters, brick makers, smiths, and metalworkers. Household goods and cloth were made by weavers, tanners, dyers (who used dye to add colors to cloth), and potters. Tan-ners produced leather for belts, shoes, bags, and harnesses for animals. Every household had a full range of pottery to store oils, grains, spices, and dried herbs. People brought water from community wells to their homes in large pottery urns.

Babylonians recognized the importance of skilled craftsmen. This was long before the time of mass manufacturing, so every pot, pan, plate, bed, and even chariot, was made individually. Craftsmen made the weapons used in war, most of the goods found in homes, and the jewelry and clothes of the *awilum*.

The Babylonians became experts at casting metal (shaping liquid metal in molds) using three different methods: open mold, closed mold, and lost wax. Metal workers used these methods for making copper and bronze items, such as spearheads, bowls, and cups. Open mold and closed mold casting means making a mold or shape, into which heated liquid metal is poured. When the metal has cooled and hardened, the mold is removed and the result is a metal object in the shape of the mould. Lost wax required making a model from wax and creating a mould from the model.

Pottery and making objects from clay were also valued skills in Baby-lonian times. Pots, bowls, and dishes were needed in every home, from a slave's house to a king's palace. People used large jars to store grain, wine, and oil. They baked meat, poultry, and fish in pottery baking dishes.

CONNECTIONS

Lost Wax Casting

Lost wax casting is still used today to make complex objects from metal. To begin, the form of the finished object is sculpted in wax. The wax form is an exact model of the item that needs to be cast in metal. So, for example, if the shape is a small statue, the wax model looks exactly the way the metal statue will look.

In Babylonian times, a coating of clay was then put over the wax. (Today, plaster or various synthetic materials are used.) This hard mold has holes at the top and bottom. The metal worker then places the clay form in sand and heats it. The wax melts and drains out the bottom of the clay form. What is left is a mold made from the wax model.

Next, the hole in the bottom of the mold is plugged with clay. Then, molten metal is poured into the space where the wax was. When the metal cools, the hard mould is chipped away, leaving a perfect metal model.

This painted pottery vase is made to look like a lion.

Some drank wine or juice from pottery cups. Some pots were highly decorated, while others were quite plain. Since clay was a common item in Babylonia, potters always had plenty of material to work with.

Babylonian homeowners stored water in large, unglazed pottery jars. Fresh water had to be hauled from the river each day. In most homes, slaves did this work. An unglazed jar offered an advantage to homeowners. It allowed water to slowly seep out through the pores in the clay. When the water reached the surface of the jar, it evaporated. Evaporation kept the water cool, which made drinking it more pleasant in the hot Babylonian climate

Some storage jars were lined with bitumen, an oily substance that oozed up through cracks in the earth's surface. Bitumen could be found naturally in a liquid and a solid form. It was used to make a waterproof seal, much in the same way that tar is used. The Babylonians used it in construction and as a way to plug leaks in farm irrigation systems.

When a storage jar was lined with bitumen, this sealed the inner surface so it did not leak or let in water vapor. This was important in storing grain, which had to be kept dry so that it did not rot. Other jars held oil. Oil was important for lighting rooms with small lamps. A lamp could be as small as a cup. Add oil and a wick, and the result is a lamp that casts about as much light as a candle.

One of the most critical occupations in Babylonia was that of the brick maker. As was true in most of Mesopotamia, there was little wood, stone, or metal for building. The city relied on brick makers to produce the required building materials for houses, businesses, and temples.

Bricks were made by mixing clay, water, and straw, and pouring it into a mould. Poor-quality bricks were then dried in the sun. The average home was made of sun-dried bricks that were produced in the month of Simanu, officially, the month of bricks. This was around our May or June, when the conditions for making bricks was ideal. The clay was wet from spring rains and the sun was hot enough to bake the bricks.

Unfortunately, sun-dried bricks were not an ideal building material. They fell apart when heavy rains came. If there was a flood, sun-dried bricks disintegrated and washed away with the water. The best bricks were kiln-baked and they were expensive. It took longer to make kiln-baked bricks. A kiln required an oven and fuel, while sun-dried bricks could be molded and lined up out in the yard until they dried.

Kiln-baked bricks were used for the outer walls of temples and palaces. No ordinary person could afford to use kiln-baked bricks for a home. Even the brick maker used sun-dried bricks for his own home. He could not afford to use kiln-baked bricks when he could earn so much more by selling them.

Kiln-baked could also be dyed to create colored bricks or glazed for a shiny, polished look. Temples, palaces, and city gates frequently featured glazed blue bricks that had the same look as polished lapis lazuli—a blue stone popular in Mesopotamia.

Ancient Boats

Iraqis who live in the marshlands of the Tigris and Euphrates Rivers today continue to make boats out of bundles of reeds tied together, in the traditional manner used more than 3,000 years ago.

The Hanging Gardens of Babylon

The Hanging Gardens of Babylon were one of the Seven Wonders of the Ancient World—seven human-made structures that were considered remarkable for their beauty and difficulty to build. This raised, terraced garden was probably built as a gift to Nebuchadnezzar's wife, Amyitis (dates unknown). Amyitis was the daughter of the king of the Medes, an ancient culture from Iran. Like many princesses, she was married to Nebuchadnezzar to form a bond between two nations. She came from the mountains and, perhaps, missed the cool, green lands of her home.

The king tried to recreate the lush green of Amyitis's homeland by creating a fake mountain covered with gardens. According to people who visited the site in ancient times, the gardens measured about 400 feet square and were 80 feet high.

It is important to understand that the hanging gardens did not hang like hanging baskets of flowers do today. They were terraced (built in several offset layers, like steps) or balcony gardens with planters. Visitors to the gardens climbed a set of stairs to the top of what seemed to be a mountain, where planters held huge trees, flowers, and vines. Water from the Euphrates River was raised by a complex system of buckets, pulleys, and cords. Since Babylon was in the heart of a semi-desert, it was necessary to provide a continuous flow of water to keep the gardens healthy. The system used a chain pump that ran from the water source (the Euphrates) to the garden irrigation pool.

There is nothing remaining of the hanging gardens of Babylon, although ancient tablets tell much about the site.

Workers in the marshlands made a variety of items from the dense, strong reeds that grew there. Like clay, reeds were always available in Mesopotamia. The reeds made excellent mats and baskets. They could also be used to make lightweight boats. The boats carried one or two people, and were used for fishing or for carrying goods on the rivers.

In the arts, sculpting was very important to Babylonians. Sculptors carved small statues of wood or ivory. Many of those statues stood in temples to represent people constantly at prayer. Other sculptors worked in stone, carving large pictures into walls. These carvings are called bas relief. A third group of sculptors produced the small cylinder seals so widely used to produce signatures on legal documents. These three types of sculpting are very different. Cylinder seals required very close, small work. Ivory and wood statues were larger, and stone carving was larger still and done with a hammer and chisel.

Of course, no Mesopotamian city-state could survive without its scribes. They read laws and documents to people. They recorded sales of goods and contracts for services. The scribes also ran schools where young boys and, sometimes, girls learned to read and write.

Babylonians wrote a type of cuneiform similar to that of the Sumerians. Like the Sumerians, the Babylonians depended on a large number of scribes to do their writing. Some of the scribes worked directly for the royal court, the military, or for wealthy merchants. Scribes for hire gathered at the city gates or near the temple waiting to be hired. People who could not read or write hired these scribes to write contracts or other documents for them.

SURVEYING AND MAPS

At the beginning, all land was owned by the king or the temples. Over time, land ownership changed. The king often gave away land as a reward to his loyal nobles and military leaders. In turn, those nobles might give land to their children or sell some land.

Babylonians were very careful about land. They laid out their cities precisely, marking out buildings, streets, parks, temples, and other areas with care. Babylonia had men who worked as surveyors to measure the land, mark its boundaries, and record the change of land ownership. The name of the new owners was carved into stones that were placed as boundary markers on the land. To make sure they kept accurate track of who owned what land and which buildings, they had land registrars. These people figured out tax rates and made maps to record who owned which areas of land.

Fields were marked with pegs and ropes to determine the borders. The people who took the surveys used triangles, rectangles, squares, and circles to map the borders of the land. Within a city, Babylonians drew accurate diagrams of the inside of palaces, temples, and homes.

When mapping flat land or drawing the outlines of buildings, Babylonians used straight lines and angles to represent land. Two parallel lines with wavy lines between them sometimes represented rivers or canals. The wavy lines stood for water. Street maps had the name of streets marked on them.

The First Man

Babylonian literature is based on Sumerian literature. Most of the stories, myths, and legends are similar to those of the Sumerians. The Babylonians also collected legal documents and scientific texts. Most cities collected documents in libraries and temples, and people could go there to read them.

One of the earliest Babylonian legends was that of Adapa, the first man. Adapa was fishing when he broke the wings of the south wind. Anu called Adapa to heaven so the gods could judge him. Ea, the god of wisdom, warned Adapa not to eat or drink anything in heaven. Adapa did what he was told. He did not eat the food Anu offered him. Unfortunately, he did not realize that eating the food of the gods would have made him immortal.

The Babylonians made maps to record who owned what areas of land. This map they made of the Mesopotamian world is engraved on a tiny clay tablet. It shows Babylon in the center (the rectangle in the top half of the circle). Other places are also named, including Elam and Assyria. The top section is a cuneiform inscription describing various regions, plus great heroes and mythical beasts.

Just like contracts and lists of goods owned, maps played an important role in the Babylonian legal system. If two people claimed the same piece of land, a map drawn on a clay tablet often helped to determine the true owner.

BABYLONIAN MATH

Much like the Sumerians, the Babylonians used an advanced number system. Many mathematicians believe the Babylonian system was more complicated than the decimal system used today. The Babylonians system used 60 as a base number. It might seem that a system based on the number 60 would be much harder to use than the system used today, which is based on the number 10. However, the Babylonians only had to learn two basic symbols to produce numbers up to 60. Combining those symbols at different angles enabled the Babylonians to write all numbers in their system.

The Babylonians divided their day into 24 hours. Each hour lasted 60 minutes, and each minute had 60 seconds. This is the same format used to keep time today.

Babylonian mathematicians developed a set of tables to help people do calculations. This was similar to a modern multiplication table. Two tablets found at Senkerah, a Babylonian city on the Euphrates River, provide tables that list the squares of the numbers up to 59 and the cubes of the numbers up to 32.

When it came to algebra, the Babylonians were way ahead of the Greeks. To find the length of the hypotenuse (the longest side) of a right triangle, Babylonians used the formula $a^2 + b^2 = c^2$. This formula is known as the Pythagorean theorem after the Greek mathematician Pythagoras (ca. 569–475 B.C.E.). However, the Babylonians were using it long before Pythagoras. Although the Babylonians could work out a number of mathematical problems, they did not have a strong understanding of geometry. For example, they did not have words for geometrical terms such as angle, parallel, and perpendicular.

CONNECTIONS

Property Deeds

The Mesopotamians believed in keeping accurate records, including records of sales, production, taxes, and other business events. One of the most important records was the sale of land. Today, sales of land or homes are registered with the local government. These major sales are recorded as deeds.

In Mesopotamia, the sale of land was also recorded by the government. The record was carved onto a *kudurru*. The *kudurru* listed every possible detail of the sale, including how much silver or how many sheep, goats, or cattle made up the purchase price.

Unlike most other documents, which were written on clay tablets, *kudurrus* were often made of stone. This was an indication of how important such a sale must have been. The Mesopotamians had very little stone to work with. Their great palaces and temples were made of brick, yet a sale of land was recorded in stone. This was to create a permanent record of the sale. *Kudurrus* were kept in temples. The gods protected the record of the sale and local citizens could view the document.

Boys in school had to study math and figure out verbal problems. The problems were practical in nature, dealing with questions such as how much water was needed to water a field. For example, if five square rods of farmland produced two bushels of barley, how much land would be needed to grow 150 bushels of barley? (The answer is 375 square rods of land.)

IT'S THE LAW!

Babylonians believed in and followed the law. The reason for this lawful behavior was probably the fact that the punishment for breaking the law was severe. So, for example, if a person broke someone's leg, that person's leg was broken as punishment. Punishments also included fines, whipping, death, or banishment (being sent away from one's home country) from Babylonia. Fines ranged from three to 30 times the value of the object damaged or stolen. By far the most common punishment for crimes was death.

A person accused of committing a crime had to appear in a court of law. The courts were at the center of the Babylonian justice system. Each court had from one to four judges. The people accusing the criminal also appeared, as did any witnesses to the crime. Witnesses could present evidence in person or send it in the form of a clay tablet. If a convicted criminal felt he had not received a fair verdict, he could appeal to the king to set aside the punishment.

The basis of Babylonian law dates from the 18th century B.C.E., when King Hammurabi established a code of laws. The laws Hammurabi collected forms the oldest known legal code in history. Hammurabi's laws reveal important information about the Babylonians. For example, they explain the rights of men, women, and children. They explain what laws people must follow and what happens if they do not obey the laws.

Before Hammurabi's laws, wealthy or powerful people could make up laws and force people to follow them. Although Hammurabi's laws were harsh, they were fair. Everyone knew what the law was, and all people were treated the same under the law.

BABYLONIAN STYLE

The Babylonians and the Assyrians wore similar styles of clothes. The clothing was a slightly more stylish version of Sumerian shawls and tunics. Just as with the Sumerians, depictions of the clothing worn by Babylonians can be seen on statues and in bas relief carvings.

Both men and women wore long tunics and shawls. Each garment was cut from one long piece of material. The length of the tunic depended on the wealth of the person. Most people who belonged to the *mushkenum* class wore knee-length tunics. Members of the *awilum* wore ankle-length tunics. Both styles had short sleeves and a rounded neckline. Most people draped a shawl over their shoulders. Some shawls had fringes or tassels. Leather or metal-link belts held the shawls in place.

Wool was plentiful. Babylonians liked bright colors, and these were created using herbal dyes. Most colors were shades of yellow, brown, orange, and rose. Fabric often featured geometric patterns that were woven into the cloth, embroidered with dyed threads, or printed onto the fabric.

Spinning and Weaving

Spinning yarn and weaving cloth were highly prized crafts, because everyone needed clothing. Wool was plentiful and was used to make most garments. Flax could also be spun into fiber to make fine linen.

Cloth was produced on large looms. Some yarn was dyed to produce red, yellow, blue, and even purple cloth. Finely spun cloth was used to make tunics and shawls for nobles, priests and priestesses, and wealthy merchants. Coarser cloth provided garments for workers and slaves. Very coarse cloth was made to be used as grain sacks or bags.

Although today's yarn production is quicker and looms produce finer, smoother cloth, there is not much difference between modern textile production and that of the Babylonians. Looms are threaded with warps and wefts, which are threads that run perpendicular to each other. The yarn for weaving is carried on a shuttle.

Hairstyles were exceptionally important for well-to-do Babylonians. Most wore their hair long with many curls and ringlets. If someone had too little hair, hairdressers provided false hair that was added to make a large hairdo. It was common for the *awilum* to wear jeweled headdresses or a band of gold or silver on their hair. All this made for extremely large hairdos among the wealthy—both men and women.

Black was the favored hair color. Many people dyed their hair black to be fashionable. Most men wore long, curled beards, and these are often seen in statues of men from the time.

Jewelry was popular, and *awilum* men and women wore pins, necklaces, bracelets, and rings. Jewelry was worked in either gold or silver, often with colored stones added. Much of the jewelry was quite intricate, showing the gold- or silversmith's talents for metalwork. Some people wore hats made of felt. These were shaped like a cylinder and sat atop the head. Footwear did not change from Sumerian times; everyone wore sandals.

Material for tunics and shawls, leather for sandals, and jewelry could be purchased in the city marketplace. The goods were paid for with silver or traded for other goods or services. Every city had professional weavers, dyers, leather workers, and jewelers. Queens, kings, and princes would have a hairdresser living in the palace and on call daily. They would also have seamstresses to sew garments.

BABYLONIAN RELIGION

The Babylonians believed in many gods. In fact, there were thousands of them. However, in everyday life most people worshipped only a handful. The gods they paid attention to would be the ones who helped them in their daily lives.

Babylonian gods were often called on to control the actions of demons that plagued humans. For example, people would ask for help from spells cast through witchcraft. Gods were also expected to let their followers know about impending dangers, such as floods or locusts. Natural disasters, such as drought, floods, and earthquakes, were believed to be punishments from the gods.

Sumerians and Babylonians worshipped many of the same gods. Some had the same powers but had different names. The god Marduk, originally the patron deity of the city of Babylon, became the most important god to Babylonians. At various times, Marduk had 50 different names. He got those names by taking the place of other gods and taking over their powers and their names. Marduk had four eyes, four ears, and spewed fire from his mouth when he spoke. Marduk was also an expert magician.

Ea was the god in charge of the great seas and fertile earth. People turned to Ea to gain wisdom or for good advice. Messages from Ea were delivered through temple priests. When he said that something would happen, Ea was usually right.

Another popular Babylonian god was Shamash, the sun god, who rose from the eastern mountains with golden rays shining from his

Popular Babylonian Gods and Goddesses

Name	Areas of Responsibility
Anu	The heavens
Ea	The sea, wisdom
Ellil	Forces of nature
Ishtar	Love
Marduk	National god of Babylonia
Nabu	Scribes
Ninurta	War
Shamash	The sun and justice
Sin	Moon

shoulders. According to legend, Shamash traveled across the sky in a chariot pulled by fiery mules.

People regularly went to the temple to make sacrifices for personal reasons. They gave gifts to a specific god to gain that god's favor. For example, a young woman who wanted to get married might offer a sacrifice to Ishtar. She then expected Ishtar to find her a lover who would become her husband. A farmer would give a gift to Ea, the god of water and fertile earth, in hope of having a good crop. A soldier would look to the god of war, Nin-

Here, Shamash, the sun god, is worshipped by three small figures.

urta, to protect him in battle. In addition to personal sacrifices, priests and priestesses would offer sacrifices from the community.

The temple was the home of the gods. It was believed that the gods left the temples to see the people of their cities and villages. They visited their friends and brought good luck to many. To celebrate the generosity of the gods, the people held festivals and celebrations. When harvest time came, the people held a festival of thanksgiving. A similar festival took place each spring when the sheep were sheared to harvest their wool.

The most important festival of the year for Babylonians was the New Year festival, called Akitu. This was an 11-day event that took place in the month of Nisan, the first month of the Babylonian calendar. (Nisan would be late March and early April in today's calendar.)

During the New Year celebration, actors presented a version of the Babylonian creation myth. The people rejoiced in the retelling of how Marduk helped in the creation of their world. Toward the end of the ceremony, the king entered the temple. He would give up his royal scepter, so he entered the temple with no symbol of his kingship. The king was then slapped very hard and embarrassed—it was important that the king had tears in his eyes. The purpose of this was to remind the king that even he had committed sins. The king would then hear a prediction about the coming year and receive his scepter back.

The Babylonian Planetary System

The Babylonians recognized seven heavenly bodies that they referred to as planets: the moon (Sin), the sun (Shamash), Jupiter (Merodach), Venus (Ishtar), Saturn (Ninip), Mercury (Nebo), and Mars (Nergal). Each planet presided over various months in the Babylonian calendar. Sin, the moon, was master of the calendar, since the calendar was based on the cycles of the moon. Sin also controlled the third month. Ninip controlled the fourth month, while Ishtar guided the sixth month.

Each planet was also connected to a specific color. The moon was silver, while the sun was gold. Mars was red, Saturn was black, and Jupiter was orange. Venus was yellow, while Mercury was blue.

The statues of the gods were washed and dressed in clean clothing. The entire city enjoyed a holiday with parades, feasts, and songs.

DEATH IN BABYLONIA

Babylonians died in many ways. They caught diseases, died in battle, and had accidents. When people died, they were given many gifts to take with them into the afterlife. A woman would be buried with cloth, perfumed oils, and jewelry. Men would receive weapons, tools, and other valuable items. The wealthier the dead person, the more valuable the items placed in the grave. A poor woman who weaved, for example, might have been buried with just cloth and the tools of her trade. A priest might be buried with a silver glass, a jar of wine, food, gold, gems, and a small statue of the god he served. All the dead would be buried with gifts of food, grain, household goods, and wine or beer for their long journey.

The *awilum* were wrapped in fine cloth and placed in a coffin for burial. *Mushkenum* and *wardum* were also wrapped, although their bodies may have been buried in coarse cloth or woven reeds. Burial took place in either the public cemetery in a burial place under the floor of the house. Funerals included special songs and mourners pounding on their chests to show their grief.

Family and friends mourned their dead for seven days. Mourners dressed in drab clothing made of coarse cloth. They were not supposed to bathe for the entire week. Many also ate very little or nothing at all for a day or more during the mourning period. A wealthy or royal family might hire professional mourners to fulfill their duties.

The dead went to a place called the netherworld. It was a place beneath the surface of the earth and was the home of ghosts and spirits. This was neither heaven nor hell, but simply a place where the dead lived after their life on earth ended.

DEMONS AND GHOSTS

The Babylonians believed that the gods affected every aspect of their lives. They also believed that demons were everywhere. Demons often

IN THEIR OWN WORDS

The Babylonian Creation Myth

This version of the Babylonian story of creation was written on seven clay tablets, each with about 150 lines of poetry. The myth is in the form of an epic poem rather than a story. The poem was written in the Akkadian language some time during the 12th century B.C.E. The tablets were found in the ruins of Ashurbanipal's palace at Nineveh in the mid-1800s by Sir Austen Henry Layard.

The myth is basically a story of the cycle of seasons. Traditionally, the epic poem was recited on the fourth day of the Babylonian New Year festival. Here is an excerpt. It tells of a time before the gods, when nothing yet had a name and all things were mingled together with no separate identities.

When on high the heaven had not been named,
Firm ground below had not been called by name,
When primordial Apsu, their begetter,
And Mummu-Tiamat, she who bore them all,
Their waters mingled as a single body,
No reed hut had sprung forth, no marshland had appeared,
None of the gods had been brought into being,
And none bore a name, and no destinies determined—
Then it was that the gods were formed in the midst of heaven.

(Source: Bratcher, Dennis. translator, *Enuma Elish*. Available online. URL: http://www.cresourcei.org/enumaelish.html. Accessed March 21, 2008.)

gathered in groups of seven and were most likely to be met in the desert. Logically, the desert was a dangerous place to be, and, for Babylonians, the presence of demons made the desert even worse. Other places people were likely to find demons included cemeteries and empty, tumbled-down buildings.

CONNECTIONS

The Zodiac

Astrology and the signs of the zodiac date back to Babylonian times. The current zodiac originated in Babylonia but changed as it was used by the Hittites, then the Phoenicians, and finally the Greeks.

Babylonian astronomers believed that the sun traveled through the sky much the way a bird flies from one place to the next. They also noticed that, at different times of the year, the sun traveled along slightly different paths. The Babylonians divided those paths into 12 groups or signs. They connected the signs with constellations that could be seen in the night sky during each period.

BABYLONIAN ZODIAC SYMBOL	MODERN ZODIAC SYMBOL	MODERN ZODIAC DATES
Laborer or messenger	Aries, the ram	March 21–April 19
A divine figure, the bull of heaven	Taurus, the bull	April 20–May 20
The faithful shepherd with twins side by side	Gemini, the twins	May 21–June 21
Crab or scorpion	Cancer, the crab	June 22–July 22
Big dog or lion	Leo, the lion	July 23–August 22
Ishtar, the virgin's ear of corn	Virgo, the virgin	August 23–September 22
Balance scales	Libra, the balance scales	September 23–October 23
Scorpion of darkness	Scorpio, the scorpion	October 24–November 21
Man or man-horse with a bow	Sagittarius, the archer	November 22–December 21
Ea's goat-fish	Capricorn, the goat	December 22–January 19
God with water urn	Aquarius, the water bearer	January 20–February 18
Fish tails in a canal	Pisces, the fish	February 19–March 20

Demons could appear in many forms. They might look like a fox or a group of dogs. They could be snakes or bats or any creature they chose. It was almost impossible for people to protect themselves from demons. Everyone knew that a demon could climb in a window, slip under the door, or arrive on the wind. Meeting up with a demon could mean illness or bad luck. If a crop failed, that might have been the work of demons. If a woman could not have children, that too could be blamed on demons.

In general, anything bad that happened in life might have happened because demons were playing evil tricks or because the gods had been angered. This left very few options for Babylonians. They had to worship their gods or suffer the consequences. There was no question that a person who suffered a string of hardships was out of favor with the gods.

Ghosts were a slightly different matter. Women in the family were responsible for honoring deceased relatives. They left water, bread, soup, beer, flour, and other items for ghosts to use. These items were left on the place where the dead were buried, which was usually under the floor of the house. The woman called the name of the dead person, then left the goods.

People expected ghosts to be pleasant spirits who helped out the family. If the ghosts were unhappy or were not well provided for, they might do something horrible to the family. So it was always a good idea to keep the ghosts happy.

Mostly, ghosts had to stay in the netherworld, the place where the dead live. A few times a year, ghosts could leave their place in the afterlife to visit friends and relatives. One of these events occurred during the late spring. These were times of celebration for a family. They entertained their ghost friends and relatives with food and drink. Afterward, the ghosts traveled back to their home among the dead. To represent this journey, the family floated boats down the river to the place of the dead, the netherworld.

CHAPTER 6

ASSYRIAN CULTURE

THE ASSYRIANS, PARTICULARLY THOSE WHO RULED DURING the last four hundred years of their empire, have had a reputation throughout history as brutal and ruthless warriors. However, remains show that they also had a strong interest in literature and scholarship, as exemplified by the library that Ashurbanipal collected in Nineveh. The Assyrians also had a long-term influence on the entire culture of the Middle East through their conquests.

Assyrian culture shared many of the features of the earlier Sumerian and Akkadian cultures. In the ancient Assyrian Empire, daily life centered on the family. The husband was the head of the household. All Assyrian men and women—from the king to a slave—were expected to marry and to produce children, particularly sons. Daughters were not as important because when they got married, they became members of their husband's families. A married daughter no longer had a connection to her birth family.

THE SOCIAL STRUCTURE

As with Sumer and Babylonia, Assyria was made up of city-states. Many people chose to live in the cities, because city life was safer. It was a period when armies of other empires could invade at any time. Cities had high walls to keep out invaders and to protect their people. And the king's army, when it was not off fighting a war, lived within the city walls.

All city dwellers were associated with a neighborhood temple. Some cities were small and had only one temple. Other cities were

OPPOSITE

The Assyrians capture an Egyptian city by using a ladder to get over the city walls.

This relief shows gangs of slaves moving a huge stone bull set on a sled to a building site.

much larger and had several different temples. Temple life was much like family life. The priests and priestesses were like parents to the people who were associated with the temple: What the priests said was the rule the temple members followed. The priests arranged work, made sure their people were fed, and saw to the needs of the community. Priests treated temple members like children—and like respectful children, the people did what they were told.

In the same way that a temple organization was like a family, so was the political organization of the king to his people. The king lived in the palace and was much like an Assyrian father. The king was the absolute authority, and the children—his subjects—did what they were told. In the same way that a father protected his family, the king protected his subjects. He raised, supplied, and led the army that defended the people from invaders.

It was also the king's duty to make sure the temples were cared for. He appointed high priests and priestesses to run the temples. He supplied slave labor to beautify the temples and build such things as city walls, canals, and roads.

Social classes were rigidly determined in Assyrian society. At the top of the social order was the king, followed by princes, then other nobles, priests, and military leaders. The middle class consisted of a variety of workers, including craftsmen, farmers, herdsmen, and merchants. These people were free men and women.

There were also slaves. People could be born slaves (they were the children of slaves), become slaves because they could not pay a debt, endure slavery as a punishment for a crime, or be captured in war. Slaves were allowed to marry, be witnesses in a trial, run a business, and own property.

WOMEN IN ASSYRIA

Women were completely dependent on their male relatives. Women raised the children and cared for the home. An old Assyrian saying was that a woman went from being a daughter to a wife, a mother, then a grandmother. In other words, she was never an independent person, free to choose her path in life.

A woman lived with her family until she married. The choice of a husband was important, and it was never left to the bride. The bride's and groom's fathers got together and agreed to a marriage. The bride may have been asked if she liked her future husband, but she was not really given a choice about whom she married. Both fathers provided gifts for the new household. The bride received a dowry from her father. The groom paid a bride price for the privilege of marrying.

Within the marriage, husband and wife had set roles. The husband was supposed to work to provide for his family. The wife was supposed to have many children, most of whom would, they hoped, be boys.

If a marriage did not work for any reason, the husband could send his wife away. If he chose to do this, he had to pay her to leave. Women did not have the freedom to leave their husbands, though.

Reading the Past

When archaeologists found thousands of tablets written in cuneiform, there was no one who could read them. These records were all carefully preserved without any idea of what they said. A tablet might have been a treaty between two warring empires or a list of goods for sale in a market.

During the 1850s, four brilliant scholars —Frenchman Jules Oppert (1825–1905), Irishman Edward Hincks (1792–1866), and two Englishmen, William Henry Fox Talbot (1800–1877) and Sir Henry Rawlinson (1810–1895)— were each given a copy of an inscription of Tiglathpileser I. This document was a reproduction of cuneiform writing found on an arti-fact excavated from Ashur (the modern city of Qalat Sherqat). The four men were asked by the Asiatic Society, a group of people interested in Mesopotamian archaeology, to work separately and translate the inscription. When they finished, the results were nearly alike. The fact that they all came up with basically the same answer showed that they were correct. The mystery of the Assyrian language was now revealed.

Since that time, historians have gained a greater understanding of the Assyrian language and have translated thousands of ancient texts.

A runaway wife or one who cheated on her husband with another man was severely punished. In some cases, the wife was stoned to death.

Some married women became slaves because of their husbands' money problems. Slavery to pay a debt was common, and a wife could be sold as a slave to pay off what her husband owed.

IN THEIR OWN WORDS

The Wife Auction

The Greek historian Herodotus (484–425 B.C.E.) toured Mesopotamia toward the end of Assyrian rule. In his book *The Histories*, written around 440 B.C.E., Herodotus said that long ago, Mesopotamian men found wives by buying them at an auction.

Once a year, in every village, this is what they used to do. They used to collect all the young women who were old enough to be married and take the whole lot of them all at once to a certain place. A crowd of men would form a circle around them there. An auctioneer would get each of the women to stand up one by one, and he would put her up for sale. He used to start with the most attractive girl there, and then, once she had fetched a good price and had been bought, he would go on to auction the next most attractive one. They were being sold to be wives, not slaves. All the well-off . . . men who wanted wives would outbid one another to buy the good-looking young women, while the commoners who wanted wives and were not interested in good looks used to end up with some money as well as the less attractive women. . . . [N]o one was allowed to take a girl he has just bought back home without first taking a pledge; he had to pledge that he would indeed live with her. . . . If they did not get
on, the rule was that the man returned the money.

According to Herodotus, the purpose of the auction was to get all the girls husbands. Pretty girls had no trouble finding husbands, but homely girls were not as lucky. However, the auction helped those who were not pretty. The money earned from the sale of good-looking brides went to provide dowries for girls who were not as attractive. A poor husband willingly married an unattractive bride who came with a good dowry. By the time Herodotus visited the region, he said bride auctions were no longer being held.

It is important to understand that Herodotus did not personally see everything he described. He often got information by interviewing others, and did not always check the accuracy of his facts. He also wrote about everything from the point of view of a Greek man who thought his own country's customs were best. Historians today do not accept everything he wrote as 100 percent true.

(Source: Herodotus. *The Histories*, Translated by Robin Waterfield. Oxford, U.K.: Oxford University Press,1998.)

This ivory sculpture shows the head of an Assyrian woman with an elaborate hairstyle topped by a hat.

The highest-status woman was the queen. Queens had their own households and managed a number of servants. However, queens were usually only valued if they gave birth to princes. They may have led more comfortable lives than the average Assyrian woman, but their basic job was the same—giving birth to the next generation.

The palace women lived in what was called a harem, but it was not like the harems that appeared later in Arabian cultures. The women of the Assyrian harem were not married to the king and did not have any type of relationship with the king. Historians do not know the reason women lived in the palace, but that is not surprising. In Assyrian culture of the time, men were important and women were not. Very little information was written about the activities of women.

Historians do know that women were limited to a specific part of the palace, and they spent much of their time doing nothing. This led to

A Legendary Queen

King Shamshi-Adad V (r. ca. 823–811 B.C.E,) had a wife who was admired throughout the land for her beauty and wisdom. He had a stele carved to honor this wife, who was named Semiramis (r. ca. 811-808 B.C.E., also written as Sammuramat or Shamiram). After Shamsi-Adad V died, she ruled Assyria for three years for her son before her son was old enough to rule on his own.

Semiramis is remembered as a brilliant military leader, and she conquered many cities. She was so widely admired that many people believed her to be a goddess. According to Assyrian legend, after Semiramis's reign she turned into a dove and flew away. Other legends claim she was killed by her own son. The stele in her honor (quoted in *Brief History of Assyrians*) says:

Stele of Sammurammat
Queen of Shamshi-Adad
King of all, king of Ashur
Mother of Adad-nerari
King of all, king of Ashur,
Daughter-in-law of Shalmaneser
King of the four regions!

This stele is one of the few artworks dedicated to a woman, although it mostly refers to her in terms of her husband, son, and father-in-law. However, the name Shamiram is remembered. Today, many Assyrian girls bear the name of this most unusual queen.

the normal problems that exist when people live in a confined area and have nothing to keep them busy. The women of the harem gossiped, bickered, and held petty grudges. In many ways, they were not too different from the kings and nobles, who, on a greater scale, bickered and squabbled with their neighbors.

For a woman, being a priestess was an important job. Priestesses usually worked in temples that honored goddesses. They performed the same jobs as priests, including running the temple business and overseeing temple lands. Priestesses took part in religious ceremonies, chanting and offering sacrifices to honor the goddess they served.

A NATION OF WARRIORS

If there was one feature of the Assyrian empire that identified the people, it was their love of war. Assyria was one of the world's first great military powers. The army was power-ful, aggressive, and cunning. Soldiers were trained to show no mercy, and their kings delighted in brutal, bloody victories. This was not unusual at the time. Most soldiers killed all those whom they met in battle.

Warlike people develop tools of war. Among the weapons the Assyrians used were iron spears, swords, shields, and armor. They added metal to the ends of battering rams (heavy beams used to break down gates or doors) to add strength. Their arrows had iron-tipped heads, which made them more deadly. The Assyrians also planned and executed successful sieges using siege towers (moveable towers with ladders inside, used to get over castle or fortress walls) and battering rams.

Assyrian soldiers in this relief carry spears and bows and arrows.

The Assyrians had chariots drawn by two horses; each chariot carried a driver and an archer (someone who shoots a bow and arrow). The Assyrians practiced with bows and arrows and were known as accurate archers. A skilled archer could kill an enemy soldier more than 270 yards away. Archers carried 50 or more arrows with them into battle.

Other weapons used by the infantry (soldiers who fight on foot) included spears and swords. The Assyrian army combined cavalry (soldiers who fight on horseback), infantry, archers, and accurate slingshots for hurling stones, and it was a deadly combination.

The Assyrians used their military skills to defeat other empires and enslave the conquered people. Historians know a great deal about Assyrian victories because they used sculpture to record their con-quests and cultural celebrations. Many of the great Assyrian bas-relief sculptures are murals dedicated to war. They show kings decorating their chariots with severed heads. They portray themselves as victori-ous heroes and the defeated peoples as slaves.

FOOD AND DRINK

For most Assyrians, bread or porridge and onions formed their basic diet. According to historical records, bread was sold by weight, rather

CONNECTIONS

Assyrian Food in America

Descendants of the ancient Assyrians keep up the traditions and customs of that culture in many places around the world. The Assyrian Cultural Center of Bet Nahrain in Ceres, California, has held an Assyrian Food Festival for more than a decade. Hundreds of people attend the event, and the main attraction is, of course, the food. A typical menu features *ricca* (baked rice), *lula kebab* (ground beef kabob), *ktaita* (chicken), *bademjohnta* (grilled tomato), and *lakh-ma* (bread). Sweets include baklava (honey and nut pastry) and halvah (a candy made with sesame seeds).

This recipe is included in *Recipes Donated by the Ladies of Chicago Assyrian Presbyterian Church*.

Lula Kebab

2 pounds ground beef chuck
1 egg
1 tablespoon plain yogurt
1 large onion, finely minced
1/4 cup green pepper, finely minced
1/4 cup fresh dill, finely minced
1 tsp seasoning salt
1/2 tsp black pepper, ground
1/2 tsp Accent

Mix all ingredients very well in a medium bowl. Work mixture into 2-inch meatballs and fix on skewers. Arrange two to four meatballs on each skewer. Cook on grill over medium heat. Serve with rice and a combination of chopped scallions, thinly sliced cucumbers, and warmed pita bread.

than by the loaf. However, the term "bread" may have meant any cooked flour product. So, for example, it could include hot cereal made of barley or wheat, similar to oatmeal or cream of wheat.

Baked bread in Assyria was not much different from bread sold in the Middle East today. Assyrian bread resembled pita bread, a pancake-shaped, flat bread baked in a hot brick oven. Bread was made of ground emmer wheat, barley, flax, and other grains and was eaten every day.

Protein in the Assyrian diet came from fish, meat, and poultry. Fish was mostly freshwater fish caught in local rivers. The Assyrians also raised fish in the ponds created by dams on the Tigris and Euphrates Rivers. Assyrians ate fish fresh or dried. Small fish were laid in the sun to dry, but a large fish was cleaned and hung on a line like laundry. Eventually, the sun and the hot, dry air dried the fish.

Meats included beef, pork, lamb, and mutton. Meat was very expensive and only wealthy Assyrians could afford to eat it regularly. The Assyrians roasted, grilled, stewed, or dried their meat. They also raised poultry and caught wild birds who lived by the water, such as ducks.

Most Assyrians drank water, wine, or beer. There were also fruit juices, but they were expensive and required more effort than just eating the fruit whole. Milk was not as common a beverage, because there was no way to store milk at a cool temperature to keep it from going sour.

A fancy Assyrian feast might also include lentils or beans, and vegetables such as pumpkins, cucumbers, and leeks. The fruits most commonly eaten were melons, pomegranates, apples, pears, apricots, plums, figs, and dates. Apricots, plums, figs, and dates could be dried to eat later. Pistachio nuts added both flavor and protein to foods. For Assyrians with a sweet tooth, cakes were baked and sweetened with honey, date syrup, or fig syrup.

WHAT THEY WORE

Assyrian men and women dressed in tunics made from a single length of cloth. They wrapped the long cloths around their bodies and fixed the material with leather belts. By 1400 B.C.E., the Assyrians had begun adding fringes to decorate their tunics. The fringed ends of the cloth hung in front, between the legs. Wealthy people also had their clothes embroidered.

In addition to tunics, some Assyrians also wore skirts that resembled Scottish kilts. The skirts were made from long swatches of cloth that were wrapped around the body. The entire arrangement—tunic and skirt—was fixed in place with a belt. For the wealthy, a jeweled pin or several were sometimes added to keep the cloth in place. In winter, a wool cloak might be worn to keep out the cold.

While Sumerians and Babylonians usually wore sandals, Assyrians usually did not. Most Assyrians went barefoot. On the rare occasions when Assyrians did wear something on their feet, they wore sandals made of a leather sole and a few leather straps to hold the shoe in place. Hunters and some warriors wore boots, but most Assyrians even went to war in their bare feet.

It was the Assyrian custom for women to wear their hair piled on their head with a bun on top. Some noble women added hair bands or pins made of gold or silver for decoration. Men also wore elaborate hairdos, with their hair long at the back and rows of braiding or curls on top. Beards on noblemen were full, long, and either curled or braided.

Everyone who could afford to do so wore jewelry. The Assyrians used ornate pins to hold their clothing. They wore pins, bands, and jeweled headdresses on their hair. Rings were common, as were bracelets,

Hats as Status Symbols

Hats or caps were often a way to tell a person's occupation or status in life. Only kings wore horn-shaped hats, since a horn was considered a symbol of power. Caps made of netting could be found on musicians and artists. Poorer men wore caps made of felt or wool.

earrings, and necklaces. Wearing a great deal of jewelry was a sign that the wearer was wealthy. The wealthier the owner, the more elaborate the jewelry. Gold, silver, and copper were common jewelry metals, and many pieces feature gems stones such as agate (black, white, or orange), lapis lazuli (blue), carnelian (red), jasper (red), and ivory or shells (yellow or white). Designs often featured circles or wheels, leaves, cones, spirals, and clusters of grapes. Cylinder seals were sometimes strung on chains and worn like jewelry.

MEDICINE IN MESOPOTAMIA

When Mesopotamians became sick, they could choose between two different types of medicine: magical medicine and physical medicine. Medical magicians or magical doctors were called *ashipu*. Physical or practical doctors were called *asu*.

The average Mesopotamian believed the cause of stomachaches, headaches, and other mysterious aches was a demon in the body. The remedy was to call an *ashipu* for a cure. That cure might be a magical charm or spell to drive away whatever demon was causing the problem.

An *ashipu* might also refer a patient to an *asu*, a healer. An *asu* could fix a broken arm, tend a serious wound, or prescribe an herbal remedy. Herbal remedies included mixtures the patient would drink or rubs placed on wounds. Most drugs were plant extracts, spices, and/or herbs mixed with sesame oil.

One of the world's first prescriptions was written for healing an infection. It was, of course, written on a clay tablet. The prescription contained turtle shells, salt, and mustard seeds. The wound had to be washed thoroughly with a rinse of beer and hot water, then rubbed with the prescription. Add some oil and a wrap made of pounded pine bark, and the infection would, hopefully, be cured.

An *asu* who performed surgery took a huge risk. If a noble or other important person was cured by an operation, the surgeon's fee was high. If an important patient died, the surgeon risked having his hand cut off.

ASSYRIAN LITERATURE

Possibly the most significant work of Assyrian literature was the epic poem *Erra and Ishum*. This work was most likely passed down through oral tradition (spoken history, such as a story passed from person to person). The best-known version was most likely written down in about 700 B.C.E.

The poem represents the typical characteristics of Assyrian culture. War and military heroics were highly valued. The hero, Ishum, is referred to as a warrior who slaughtered many and was highly successful.

IN THEIR OWN WORDS

Erra and Ishum

The Assyrian people believed that their gods had very human characteristics. Some gods were warlike, while other gods were friendly. Some were hard working, while others were lazy. This story is the epic of Erra, a lazy god. In this story, seven unnamed gods complain to Erra and encourage him to act on their behalf. Erra is tired and needs a thorough scolding to get him to act.

The Seven [gods] claim vaguely that they are not respected enough, that others are growing more important than they are. They bring up the old charge that men make too much noise for the gods to sleep, although this was not the cause Erra had given for his own lack of sleep.

The Seven claim further that there are too many wild animals on the loose. Their final claim, no doubt the most important one, is that they are bored and out of training. These are the ones who are in a fury, holding their weapons aloft, They are saying to Erra:

"Up, do your duty!

Why have you been sitting in the city like a feeble old man,

Why sitting at home like a helpless child?

Shall we eat woman food, like noncombatants? Have we turned timorous and trembling, as if we can't fight?

Going to the field for the young and vigorous is like to a very feast,

But the noble who stays in the city can never eat enough.

His people will hold him in low esteem, he will command no respect, . . .

However toothsome city bread, it holds nothing to the campfire loaf,

However sweet fine beer, it holds nothing to water from a skin, . . .

Be off to the field, warrior Erra, make your weapons clatter,

Make loud your battle cry that all around they quake,

Let the Igigi-gods hear and extol your name,

Let the Anunna-gods hear and flinch at the mention of your,

Let all the gods hear and bend for your yoke,

Let sovereigns hear and fall prostrate before you,

Let countries hear and bring you their tribute,

Let the lowly hear and perish of their own accord,

Let the mighty hear and his strength diminish,

Let lofty mountains hear and their peaks crumble, . . .

Let the gods your ancestors see and praise your valor!"

(Source: Foster, B. *Distant Days: Myths, Tales, and Poetry from Ancient Mesopotamia.* Bethesda, Md.: CDL Press, 1995.)

The Assyrians worshipped thousands of gods. This one is a warrior god.

THE ASSYRIAN GODS

Assyrian religion, like that of other Meso-potamian cultures, recognized many gods. Each area of life had a god responsible for its success or failure. There were also major gods and minor gods. In hard times, the Assyrian people asked their chosen god or goddess to help resolve their problems. The people knelt before their gods and bowed to them, making themselves humble. They also offered up sac-rifices to please their chosen gods.

The Assyrians worshipped thousands of gods, but there were about 20 major gods. Those gods were recognized by everyone as important. Other gods had less importance and, therefore, less power. They might be gods of just a small region or a single place, for example.

The primary god, Ashur held the great-est importance. In fact, the word *Assyrian* comes from the name Ashur, the main Assyrian god. The capital city of the Assyr-ian Empire was named for this god. He served as the Assyrian national patron and the god of the universe. Ashur was believed to be the most powerful of gods.

The Assyrians also had gods that they related to stars, planets, and other heavenly bodies. Shamash was the sun god, while Sin was the moon god. Ishtar, in addition to being the goddess of love and war, was also the goddess of the morning and evening stars.

Some Assyrian gods originally came from the Sumerians or the Babylonians. These gods, such as Anu, Ellil, Ishtar, and Ea, were patrons of the oldest cities. While many cultures tried to wipe out the religion of the people they conquered, the Assyrians did not. They accepted that the gods of Sumer and Babylonia were important and worshipped them as such.

Newer gods also had places in the Assyrian temples. They were usually patrons of newly built cities, weather events, or common occur-rences. For example, Adad was the Assyrian god of storms. He brought rain, which was good. He also brought thunder and lightning, which were not quite as good. When Adad brought too much rain, there were floods, which were definitely not good at all. The Assyrians believed that problems such as drought or floods showed that the gods were angry. A light rain that helped the crops meant that the gods were happy.

THE GODS' TEMPLES

Assyrian temples were huge, multi-purpose buildings with many rooms. Priests conducted religious rituals in them every day. Large temples had open courtyards with fountains used for washing and altars for animal sacrifices. Every temple had rooms where the gods themselves lived.

A god was represented by a statue, which was usually quite large and frightening. The average person never entered the rooms of the gods. Even temple servants were not allowed into the gods' rooms. Only the high priests or priestesses and, occasionally, kings entered the most sacred areas of the temple.

The temples varied in size according to the god's importance. A truly important god had large rooms that were decorated with gold, silver, gems, and valuable wood. In his statue, he would be shown in human form and wearing fancy clothing. To make sure the people remained close to and loyal to their gods, the statues were paraded through the city on special occasions. These festivals were the few holidays that Assyrian people enjoyed and were a welcome break from the endless work of making a living.

Feasts of the Gods

The priests in Assyrian temples offered the gods three meals a day. This was much more food than the average person ate.

EPILOGUE

THE ANCIENT EMPIRES THAT FLOURISHED IN THE REGION known as Mesopotamia covered at their largest extent an area that stretched from the Mediterranean coast of modern Syria to Iraq and Iran, west of the Zagros Mountains. Most of the people who live in the area today follow the Islamic religion and consider themselves to be either Arabs or Persians.

Rulers include sheikhs and emirs, presidents and supreme leaders, but there are no kings. The borders are mostly fixed and are recognized by nations around the world. Throughout the region, oil production is the major business. The land is still very dry, and the Tigris and Euphrates Rivers provide the people with water for drinking and for irrigating crops. Damascus and Baghdad, two cities from ancient times, are now the capitals of Syria and Iraq.

FROM ANCIENT TO MODERN DAY

Politics in ancient Mesopotamia was structured in such a way that no one group of people was able to stay in power for very long. Since there was no one, clear leader to unify various areas, different cities were able to grow stronger at various times. Different groups, each with slightly different customs, religions, and languages gained and lost strength, sometimes even regaining power centuries later. As a result, the region was especially vulnerable to foreign invasions, as seen with the Persian Cyrus the Great and the Macedonian Alexander the Great.

In fact, over the course of several thousand years, Mesopotamia experienced a number of changes in power from outside influence.

OPPOSITE
Iraqis visit the restored Iraqi National Museum in Baghdad on February 23, 2009. This is the day it was formally dedicated, nearly six years after looters stole many precious objects from the museum.

After Alexander's death in 323 B.C.E. a group of people called the Parthians dominated the area, who were originally from the area now called Iran. Eventually the rule passed to the Sassanian Persians, also from Iran. The Sassanians were able to maintain their hold on the area from the third century C.E. until the seventh century, when Arabs conquered the area bringing with them Islam, a religion founded by the prophet Muhammad.

The arrival of the Muslims (the name of the followers of Islam) is one of the most significant moments of this area's history. The Muslims quickly made the area their home and set up a type of government system called a caliphate. At the top of the caliphate was a single leader, known as the caliph, who was responsible for unifying the various areas of Islam that existed across the Middle East and North Africa. A particularly powerful ruling family, the Abbasid dynasty, was significantly influential in the area. In the eighth century the Abbasids built the city of Baghdad, which became the region's center for trade, education, and culture. It was not just an Islamic city. Jews, Christians, Persians, Indians, and Greeks all settled in Baghdad, which helped spread Islamic culture and knowledge around Europe and Asia. During this golden age of Islamic civilization breakthroughs in science, art, and literature became known throughout the continents. The city has not lost its importance, for today Baghdad is the capital of Iraq.

The rule of the Abbasids came to an end with the arrival of a people from Central Asia called the Mongols. Hülegü Khan, grandson of the legendary warrior Genghis Khan, led his soldiers in an attack against Baghdad in 1258 that ultimately destroyed this center of Islamic culture and political authority. Although the Mongols did not completely conquer and dominate Iraq, the Abbasids were never able to regain control. Instead, the region experienced instability and constant changes in rule until the leaders of the Ottoman Empire, which was based in the region that is now Turkey, took control in 1831.

Ottoman control lasted through the century, and ended just after the conclusion of World War I in 1918. The Ottomans had allied themselves with Germany during the war, and when they lost the war, the Ottomans lost their hold on the region. Control of Iraq passed to Great Britain, which established an authority called a mandate. This meant they were legally in power in Iraq, but they could appoint individuals to help keep the area stable. The Iraqis believed they should be ruled by a monarch, and so the British chose Faisal, former king of Syria, to act as the figurehead to the various peoples within the region.

Faisal ruled under the British until 1932, when he convinced them to grant Iraq full independence. Although still plagued by turmoil, Iraq maintained a monarchy until 1958, when it was overthrown in a revolt by the Iraqi army. Over the next two decades several groups of people fought to gain power in Iraq, but it was not until Saddam Hussein (1937–2006) became president in 1979 that the government was brought under control.

FROM MONARCH TO DICTATOR

Iraq is home to three major groups of people: the Shiites and Sunnis, two groups who follow two distinct forms of Islam, and an ethnic group called the Kurds. Most Kurds follow the Sunni faith. Shiites tend to live in the southern part of the country. Sunnis occupy the center and the west. Kurds live in the north along the border with Turkey.

In Iraq, the difference between Shiite and Sunni Muslims is a political as well as a religious division. This difference in political status has made the two groups enemies. Shiites outnumber Sunnis, but Sunnis have historically held the political and economic power.

At the time when Saddam Hussein took power in Baghdad in 1979, Iraq's Shiites enjoyed relative equality with the Sunnis. However, in 1979 there was a revolution in the neighboring Islamic country Iran, in which Shiites were able to take control of the Iranian government. After that, Hussein feared Iraqi Shiites might be encouraged to follow that example in Iraq. Iran and Iraq were at war from 1980 to 1988, and when the war ended, Shiites were pushed out of most senior government and military positions in Iraq.

Hussein continued his rule as a dictator throughout the 1990s. Tensions continued between Iran and Iraq, and between the Shiites and Sunnis. In 2003, the United States, along with several other nations, invaded Iraq. There were many reasons for this invasion. Some people believed that Hussein's government was developing weapons of mass destruction. These weapons included chemical weapons that could cause many deaths and biological weapons that

Fast Facts: Iraq

Area: 168,754 square miles)

Population: 28,946,000 (2009 estimate)

Capital City: Baghdad

People: Arab 75–80%, Kurds 15–20%, Turkomans, Assyrians

Languages: Arabic, Kurdish, Turkoman Assyrian, Armenian

Religions: Islam 97% (Shiites 60–65%, Sunnis 32–37%), Christian and other 3%

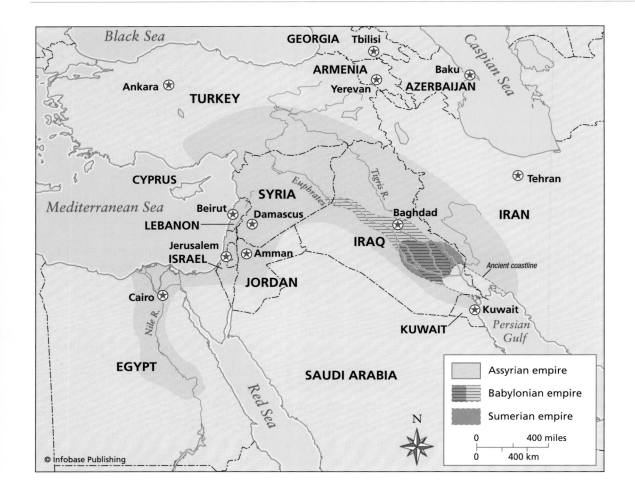

The Sumerian and Babylonian Empires stretched across south and central Iraq. The Assyrian Empire, whose capital was located in northern Iraq, ruled a vast territory that extended from western Iran and the Persian Gulf to south and central Turkey, Syria, Lebanon, Israel, Jordan, and into Egypt.

spread diseases such as anthrax. Hussein had used chemical weapons against his own people in the past to suppress rebellions against his government. Other reasons for the war were a belief that Iraq allowed terrorists to live and train there, and the knowledge that Hussein's government was abusing Iraqi citizens.

The invasion was quick and within a few months the war seemed to be over. The invasion was followed by a period of lawlessness and looting that damaged much of the country's basic services, and in many places these services have not been completely restored. Millions of dollars have been poured into Iraq to rebuild the cities, roads, and other facilities. Yet nearly one-third of all Iraqis have daily problems with their water supply. Only one in five households has a reliable sewage system.

Living in Iraq today still means living in a war zone. Fighting continues, with small bands of anti-government forces frequently attacking mostly civilian targets. More than 60,000 Iraqi civilians have died since the fighting officially ended. Attacks by suicide bombers have increased, as have the number of people dying in those bombings. Soldiers from the United States and other nations remain in Iraq.

There are sharp divisions between Shiite and Sunni, and between those who would like to see a government based on Muslim religious law and those who would like to see a secular (nonreligious) government. These divisions often result in violence. The ideas behind the war and the hopes for changing Iraq's future have been difficult to put into practice. The end result of the war is not yet clear.

Iraqis now have access to consumer goods that were not easily available before 2003. The number of people who now own cars has doubled in five years. Cell phones and satellite television dishes are hot items. Yet only five in 100 households have computers, and only slightly more own cameras. Vacuum cleaners are rare, and only one in four families own washing machines or cars.

For the Kurds in the north, life has improved. The Kurds were greatly oppressed under Hussein's government, and are now enjoying much greater freedom. They can train for and hold jobs that

Iraqi Oil

Iraq has the third largest oil reserves in the world. About three-fifths of the country's economic earnings depend on oil. This should make Iraq a very rich nation, but it does not. Under Saddam Hussein's rule, wealthy Iraqis—Hussein's supporters—became immensely wealthy, while poor Iraqis remained poor.

In 2003, when the United States and its allies invaded Iraq, oil wells and refineries became major targets for groups supporting Hussein and those opposed to the United States presence. From April 2003 to January 2007, there were nearly 400 attacks on Iraqi oil and gas pipelines, oil industry workers, and refineries. These attacks cost the country billions of dollars. Oil production is well below the nation's potential of 6 million barrels a day. From 2003 to 2009, production has never gone much beyond 2 million barrels a day.

Despite the rich oil reserves in Iraq, the oil industry is not meeting the needs of the Iraqi people. In a nation with so much oil, shortages at the gas pumps have forced many Iraqis to line up to fill their car's gas tanks.

were previously closed to them. Kurdish women also have greater rights than they did under the previous government.

ANCIENT TREASURES: LOST AND FOUND

The war in Iraq also posed a threat to the newly opened National Museum of Iraq. First opened by British archaeologist Gertrude Bell in 1926, this museum holds one of the most extensive collections of Mesopotamian history and culture in the world. The museum has artifacts dating back more than 5,000 years to the Stone Age in the Fertile Crescent.

The unstable atmosphere of this region has made it increasingly difficult to protect the building and its pieces from damage or theft. The museum first closed its doors in 1991, the first time the United States invaded Iraq during a conflict known as the Gulf War. It remained locked until April 28, 2000, when Hussein opened it on his birthday.

The 2003 U.S. invasion proved to be detrimental to the museum's treasures. Despite efforts to avoid unnecessary damage to the building and its artifacts, the museum was the site of several violent clashes between U.S. and Iraqi forces. In the chaotic months that followed, the museum was looted several times and more than 15,000 items were reported missing. UNESCO (United Nations Education, Scientific and Cultural Organization) immediately launched an international investigation to locate the missing items and return them to the museum. As of 2009, almost 6,000 artifacts have been recovered, including the invaluable Sumerian Warka Mask, the Warka Vase, and the legendary treasures of Nimrud.

On February 23, 2009, Iraqi prime minister Nuri al-Maliki once again opened the museum to a limited public. Plans have been developed to eventually allow admission to the general public, although that date is currently unknown.

One exciting discovery occurred in 2003, just after the U.S. invasion. Northern Iraq has been a popular excavation site for more than 150 years, and archaeologists have found ruins and artifacts of the Assyrians who lived there thousands of years ago. A palace complex built by Ashurnasirpal II was discovered near the Tigris River, which included four main palaces, three smaller ones, several townhouses, temples and even a ziggurat. Over the years treasures from this site, including jewelry, gold, semi-precious stones, and containers have

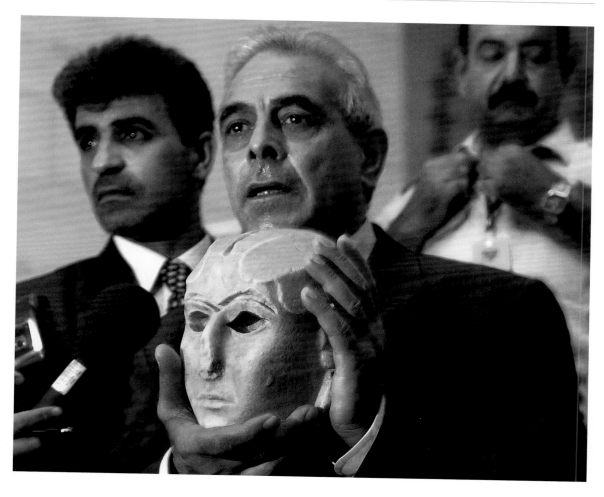

been collected and locked in the Iraqi National Bank in Baghdad. During the invasion, the bank was flooded, possibly to prevent theft by looters, and historians and archaeologists worried about the artifacts. A team from National Geographic drained more than half a million gallons of water from the underground, flooded levels in the bank to find the items were intact and unharmed. The team successfully recovered them.

The ruins of magnificent palaces and ziggurats, the intricate sculptures and pieces of pottery, and the elaborate bas-reliefs are just some of the treasures that remind the modern world of ancient civilizations. Yet the influences of ancient Mesopotamia go beyond the physical objects and artifacts collected over the centuries.

Iraqi minister of Culture Mufeed Muhammad Jawad al Jazairee holds the Warka Mask, a Sumerian artifact that was looted from the National Museum of Iraq. Iraqi police recovered the head in September 2003.

This gold crown is one of the beautiful treasures discovered at Nimrud in Iraq.

Mesopotamia is justly called the "cradle of civilization." They introduced the world to farming, which allowed the ancient people to create the first known towns and cities. They created the wheel, developed the concept of the 60-minute hour, and, perhaps the greatest contribution of all, the written word.

TIME LINE

ca. 10,000 B.C.E.	Hunter-gatherers hunt large game and harvest wild plants in the area that will become known as Mesopotamia.
ca. 9000 B.C.E.	Farming begins; animals are domesticated for farm use and crops are planted.
ca. 7000 B.C.E.	Pottery is developed to store and cook foods and liquids.
ca. 6500 B.C.E.	People build small villages in Mesopotamia.
ca. 5000 B.C.E.	The Ubaidians develop mud bricks.
ca. 4500 B.C.E.	Farmers develop plows for tilling the soil.
ca. 4000 B.C.E.	The city of Uruk is established in Sumer.
ca. 3400 B.C.E.	The development of wheeled vehicles makes transportation easier.
ca. 3200 B.C.E.	Emergence of writing.
ca. 3100 B.C.E.	The Sumerians develop bronze tools.
2900–2334 B.C.E.	The Sumerian culture thrives; cuneiform script developed.
2700 B.C.E.	A calendar is developed, dividing the year into months based on the phases of the moon.
2334 B.C.E.	King Sargon of Agade begins his reign, marking the start of the Akkadian period.
1900–1595 B.C.E.	The Old Babylonian Period
1792 B.C.E.	The Babylonian Empire rises; Hammurabi becomes king.
1755 B.C.E.	Hammurabi delivers his code of laws.
1600 B.C.E.	The Hittites invade Mesopotamia and sack Babylon in 1595 B.C.E. Their empire lasts until 1200 B.C.E.
1595–1000 B.C.E.	The Middle Babylonian Period
1365 B.C.E.	The Assyrians rise to power in Mesopotamia.
880 B.C.E.	Nimrud becomes capital of Assyria.
705 B.C.E.	The Assyrian capital moves to Nineveh.
669 B.C.E.	Ashurbanipal becomes king of Assyria.
625–539 B.C.E.	The Neo-Babylonian Period

604 B.C.E. Nebuchadnezzar II becomes king of Chaldea.

586 B.C.E. Jerusalem is destroyed by King Nebuchadnezzar II.

539 B.C.E. Cyrus the Great and his Persian army invade Mesopotamia.

GLOSSARY

alliance   a friendship or bond between two groups or nations

amelu   the upper class of Sumerian society

archaeology   the study of ancient people and cultures

artifacts   items made by humans, such as pottery or tools

astronomy   the study of how stars, planets, and other objects move in space

awilum   Babylonians who owned their own land and did not depend on the temple or the king for land to farm

bas-relief   carved sculpture in which the figures stand out from the background

caravan   a group of people traveling together, often traders

chariot   a cart with two wheels pulled by horses

city-state   a city and its surrounding farms that functions as a separate nation

clan   a group of close-knit families

culture   the religious, social, and artistic beliefs and customs of a group of people

cuneiform   a system of writing on clay tablets using a triangular writing instrument, called a stylus

cylinder seal   a tubular, carved object that presses a design into wet clay or wax; it is used in the same way as a signature

dike   a low wall, often made of earth, built to keep out water and prevent flooding

domesticated animals   animals bred for use in agriculture or to work with people

dowry   money or gifts from her family that a wife brings to her marriage

drought   a long period without rain

dynasty   a family that keeps control of a government over many generations, with rule often passed from a parent to a child

epic   a long poem about the actions and adventures of heroic or legendary figures or about the history of a nation

epidemic   widespread disease that attacks many people

famine   a period during which food is scarce

fertile   able to easily grow (for plants) or have offspring (for animals and people)

heir   the person named to inherit a title or property

hunter-gathers   people who hunt game animals, fish, and gather wild fruit, roots, nuts, and berries to feed themselves

inscription   words that are carved into a hard surface

irrigation   bringing water to crops through canals or ditches

lunar calendar   a way of recording months and days based on the cycles of the moon

midwife   a person who is trained to deliver babies but is not a doctor

mosaic   a picture or decoration made from small pieces of colored tile

mushkinu   the middle class of Sumerian society, including merchants, skilled tradespeople, and shopkeepers

mushkenum   under Hammurabi, people who worked in the palace, and more generally, members of the Babylonian upper class who worked directly for the king

nobility   the upper class of society; the members of this class are *nobles*

obelisk   a four-sided stone column that tapers to a point on top

pasha   a Middle Eastern governor

patron god   a god who is the special protector of a region or a group of people

pictograph   pictures used to represent words in a writing system

prosperity   doing well in terms of having material things

raze   to destroy to the ground, as in a building or city

reign   the period of time during which an individual ruler rules

sacred   holy

satrapy   a province of the ancient Persian government

scholar   a person dedicated to learning and study

scribe   a person who makes a living by writing down official records

shekel   a unit of currency

siege   cutting off a town or fort from the outside so it cannot receive supplies and the inhabitants cannot escape

stele   a stone pillar with an inscription on it

stylus   a writing implement made from bone, wood, metal, or reed

suq   an open-air or street market

tablet   a flat slab of stone, clay, or wood, used for writing

tell   an archaeological mound containing debris from an ancient culture

tenant farmer   a person who rents land that he or she farms for a living

tribute   a tax paid to a ruler, usually by those conquered in war

tunic   a loose garment similar in shape to a dress

wardum   a Babylonian slave or servant

ziggurat   a stepped pyramid; that is, a pyramid made of terraces like a huge set of stairs, with a flat top

BIBLIOGRAPHY

"Accounts of the Campaign of Sennacherib, 701 B.C.E." Internet Ancient History Sourcebook. Available online. URL: http://www.fordham.edu/halsall/ancient/701sennach.html. Accessed March 16, 2008.

"Ancient Mesopotamia: This History, Our History." The Oriental Institute at the University of Chicago. Available online. URL: http://mesopotamia.lib.uchicago.edu/mesopotamialife/article.php. Accessed March 16, 2008.

"Ancient Tablets, Ancient Graves: Assessing Women's Lives in Mesopotamia." Women in World History. Available online. URL: http://www.womeninworldhistory.com/lesson2.html. Accessed March 17, 2008.

Ascalone, Enrico, *Mesopotamia.* Berkeley, Calif.: University of California Press, 2007.

"Ashurbanipal." LookLex Encyclopaedia. Available online. URL: http://i-cias.com/e.o/ashurbanipal.htm. Accessed March 17, 2008.

"Babylon." EMuseum @ Minnesota State University, Mankato. Available online. URL: http://www.mnsu.edu/emuseum/archaeology/sites/middle_east/babylon.html. Accessed March 17, 2008.

"Babylonia, A history of ancient Babylon." The International History Project 2004. Available online. URL: http://www.history-world.org/babylonia.htm. Accessed March 16, 2008.

"Babylonians," Ancient Civilizations. Available online. URL: http://home.cfl.rr.com/crossland/AncientCivilizations/Middle_East_Civilizations/Babylonians/babylonians.html. Accessed March 17, 2008.

"The Banquet of Ashurnasirpal II." Wittenburg University. Available online. URL: http://www4.wittenberg.edu/academics/hist/dbrookshedstrom/105/bqtashur.htm. Accessed March 21, 2008.

Berlin, Adele, Marc Zvi Brettler, and Michael Fisbane, eds., *The Jewish Study Bible.* New York: Oxford University Press, 2004.

BetBasoo, Peter, *Brief History of Assyrians.* Available online. URL: www.aina.org/aol/peter/brief.htm#Religion. Accessed March 21, 2008.

Bottero, Jean, *Everyday Life in Ancient Mesopotamia.* Baltimore, Md.: Johns Hopkins University Press, 2001.

Bratcher, Dennis, translator, *Enuma Elish.* Available online. URL: http://www.cresourcei.org/enumaelish.html. Accessed March 21, 2008.

Brief History of Assyrians. Available online, URL: http://www.aina.org/aol/peter/brief.htm#First. Accessed January 28, 2008.

Brown, Dale M., editor, *Mesopotamia: The Mighty Kings.* New York: Time-Life Books, 1995.

Butterfield, Bruce J., *Epic of Ishtar and Izdubar.* Available online. URL: http://mcadams.posc.mu.edu/txt/ah/Assyria/Izdubar_intro.html#intro. Accessed March 21, 2008.

"The Code of the Ashura." Internet Ancient History Sourcebook. Available online. URL: http://www.fordham.edu/haslsall/ancient/1075assyriancode.html. Accessed March 21, 2008.

"Country Profile: Iran." BBC News. Available online. URL: http://news.bbc.co.uk/2/hi/middle_east/country_profiles/790877.stm. Accessed March 17, 2008.

"Country Profile: Kuwait." BBC News. Available online. URL: http://newsvote.bbc.co.uk/mpapps/pagetools/print/news.bbc.co.uk/2/hi/middle_east/country_profiles/791053.stm. Accessed March 17, 2008.

"Cyrus the Great or Cyrus the Elder." Dromo's Den. Available online. URL: http://www.dromo.info/cyrusbio.htm. Accessed March 17, 2008.

Dalley, S., "The Flood." *Myths from Mesopotamia.* Available online. URL: http://web.archive.org/web/19990221091328/http://puffin.creighton.edu/theo/simkins/tx/Flood.html. Accessed March 21, 2008.

"Dedicatory Inscription on the Ishtar Gate, Babylon." Ishtar Gate Inscription. Available online. URL: http://www.kchanson.com/ANCDOCS/meso/ishtarins.html. Accessed March 17, 2008.

Elmer-Dewitt, Philip, "The Golden Treasures of Nimrud." *Time*, October 30, 1989. Available online. URL: http://www.time.com/time/magazine/article/0,9171,958909-2,00.html. Accessed March 22, 2008.

Fattah, Hala with Frank Caso, *A Brief History of Iraq.* New York: Facts On File, 2009.

"The First Declaration of Human Rights." Persian Journal. Available online. URL: http://www.iranian.ws/cyrus.htm. Accessed March 21, 2008.

Foster, B., *Distant Days: Myths, Tales, and Poetry from Ancient Mesopotamia.* Bethesda, Md.: CDL Press, 1995.

Frankfort, Henri, *The Birth of Civilization in the Near East.* Bloomington, Ind.: Indiana University Press, 1956.

Goodspeed, George, *Assyria.* Available online. URL: http://history-world.org/assyrians.htm. Accessed March 21, 2008.

Guisepi, Robert A., *Ancient Sumeria.* Available online. URL: http://history-world.org/sumeria.htm. Accessed March 21, 2008.

Hallo, William W., and William Kelly Simpson, *The Ancient Near East: A History,* 2nd ed. New York: Harcourt Brace College Publishers, 1998.

"Hammurabi," LookLex Encyclopedia. Available online. URL: http://i-cias.com/e.o/hammurabi.htm. Accessed March 17, 2008.

Herodotus, *The Histories*, Translated by Robin Waterfield. Oxford, U.K.: Oxford University Press, 1998.

The History Files, Kingdoms of the Middle East. Available online. URL: http://www.historyfiles.co.uk/MainListsMiddleEast.htm. Accessed April 6, 2008.

"Inscription of Nebuchadrezzar," Assyrian Texts/Marquette University. Available online. URL: http://mcadams.posc.mu.edu/txt/ah/Assyria/Inscrb00.html. Accessed March 16, 2008.

"The Iraq Crisis." Global Issues/Geopolitics. Available online. URL: http://www.globalissues.org//'Geopolitics/MiddleEast/Iraq/PostWar.asp. Accessed March 21, 2008.

Kramer, Samuel Noah, *History Begins at Sumer.* State College, Pa.: University of Pennsylvania Press, 1998.

"Lack of Security and Deteriorating Conditions." Global Issues/Geopolitics. Available online. URL: http://www.globalissues.org/Geopolitics/MiddleEast/Iraq/PostWar/Security.asp?p=1. Accessed March 17, 2008.

Layard, Austen Henry, *A Popluar Account of Discoveries at Nineveh.* Available online. www.aina.org/books/dan.htm. Accessed March 21, 2008.

Leick, Gwendolyn, *The Babylonians.* London: Routledge Press, 2003.

"Life in Iraq." BBC News. Available online. URL: http://news.bbc.co.uk/2/shared/spl/hi/in_depth/post_saddam_iraq/html/1.stm. Accessed March 17, 2008.

Luckenbill, D. D., *Records of Assyria,* Vol. II. Chicago: University of Chicago Press, 1926.

Mackenzie, Donald A., *Myths of Babylonia and Assyria.* Available online. URL: http://www.gutenberg.org/etext/16653. Accessed March 21, 2008.

Malam, John, *Mesopotamia and the Fertile Crescent.* Austin, Tex.: Raintree Steck-Vaughn, 1999.

"Mesopotamia." The International History Project. Available online. URL: http://history-world.org/mesopotamia_a_place_to_start.htm. Accessed March 17, 2008.

Mesopotamian Documents. Available online. URL: http://www.kchanson.com/ANCDOCS/meso/ishtarins.html. Accessed March 16, 2008. (Based on Marzahn, Joachim, *The Ishtar Gate, The Processional Way, The New Year Festival of Babylon.* Mainz am Rhein, Germany: Philipp von Zaubern, 1995.)

"Mesopotamian Menus." Saudi Aramco World. Available online. URL: http://www.saudiaramcoworld.com/issue/198802/mesopotamian.menus.htm. Accessed March 17, 2008.

"Mesopotamian/Sumerian Calendar." The International History Project. Available online. URL: http://history-world.org/mesopotamiancalander. htm. Accessed March 16, 2008.

Mitchell, Stephen, *Gilgamesh: A New English Version.* New York: Free Press, 2006.

"My Day in Iraq: Social Worker." BBC News. Available online. URL: http://newsvote.bbc.co.uk/ mpapps/pagetools/print/news.bbc.co.uk/2/hi/middle_east/4884358.stm. Accessed March 17, 2008.

Nardo, Don, *Ancient Mesopotamia.* San Diego, Calif.: Lucent Books, 2004.

Nemet-Nejat, Karen Rhea, *Daily Life in Ancient Mesopotamia.* Westport, Conn.: Greenwood Press, 1998.

Oppenheim, Leo A.., *Ancient Mesopotamia: Portrait of a Dead Civilization*, revised ed., completed by Erica Reiner. Chicago: University of Chicago Press, 1977.

Price, Massoume, "History of Ancient Medicine in Mesopotamia & Iran," Iran Chamber Society. Available online. URL: http://www.iranchamber. com/history/articles/ancient_medicine_ mesopotamia_iran.php. Accessed March 21, 2008.

Rizza, Alfredo, *The Assyrians and the Babylonians: History and Treasures of an Ancient Civilization.* Boston: White Star Publications, 2007.

Roaf, Michael, *Cultural Atlas of Mesopotamia and the Ancient Near East.* Abingdon, U.K.: Andromeda Oxford Books, 2004.

Roth, Martha T., et al., *Law Collections from Mesopotamia and Asia Minor*, Atlanta: Scholars Press, 1995, reprint 1997.

Saggs, H. W. F., *Babylonians.* Berkeley, Calif.: University of California Press, 2000.

Sargis, Rose, "Lula Kebab." *Recipes Donated by the Ladies of Chicago Assyrian Presbyterian Church.* Available online, URL: http://www.ronjdavid.com/ assyrian_recipes.htm. Accessed February 17, 2008.

"Sargon II of Assyria." Biography Base. Available online. URL: http:// www.biographybase.com/ biography/Sargon_II_of_Assyria.html. Accessed March 17, 2008.

Schmandt-Besserat, Denise, "Signs of Life." *Odyssey,* January/February 2002. Available online. URL: http://webspace.utexas.edu/dsbay/Docs/ SignsofLife.pdf. Accessed March 17, 2008.

"Sennacherib's Campaign." Internet Ancient History Sourcebook. Available online. URL: http://www. fordham.edu/halsall/ancient/701sennach.html. Accessed March 21, 2008.

"Shining New Light on an Assyrian Palace." The Metropolitan Museum of Art—Special Exhibitions. Available online. URL: http://www.metmuseum.org/ special/ane/assyrian.html. Accessed March 21, 2008.

Speiser, E. A., translator, *Ancient Near Eastern Texts Related to the Old Testament.* Princeton, N.J.: Princeton University Press, 1969.

Thomson, R. C., *The Prisms of Esarhaddon and Ashurbanipal Found at Nineveh, 1927-8.* London: British Museum Press, 1931.

"The Tower of Babel." The Museum of Unnatural Mystery. Available online. URL: http://www.unmuseum. org/babel.htm. Accessed September 1, 2008.

"Welcome to the Library of King Ashurbanipal." University of Tennessee, Knoxville. Available online. URL: http://web.utk.edu/~giles/. Accessed March 21, 2008.

"Words of Wisdom." Women in World History. Available online. URL: http://www.womeninworldhistory. com/wisdom.html. Accessed September 1, 2008.

FURTHER RESOURCES

BOOKS

Bancroft-Hunt, Norman, *Historical Atlas of Ancient Mesopotamia* (New York: Checkmark Books, 2004)

> More than a collection of maps, this atlas provides details on the lives of the various people who lived and ruled in Mesopotamia, the birthplace of farming, the alphabet, and other key aspects of civilization. The great kingdoms before the Persian Empire—including Sumer, Akkadia, Assyria, and Babylonia—are all featured. For the Persians, the author looks at all three great dynasties, ending with the fall of the Sassanian Empire to the Arabs. Through 40 full-color maps, pictures, and text, the book highlights Persia's conflict with others and daily life in ancient Mesopotamia.

Farndon, John, *Eyewitness Mesopotamia* (New York: Dorling Kindersley, 2007)

> This book presents the history and culture of Mesopotamia using many photos and illustrations with short, informative text to support each one. The book comes with a clip-art CD and a wall chart of facts, artifacts, and events from ancient Iraq. Visit a ziggurat, learn about the rise of Babylon, or discover the art of hunting at the time when Mesopotamia was the cradle of civilization.

McCaughrean, Geraldine, *Gilgamesh the Hero* (Grand Rapids, Mich.: Eerdmans Books for Young Readers, 2003)

> This book retells the earliest epic story, the ancient legend of Gilgamesh, as a modern-day novel.

Mitchell, Stephen, *Gilgamesh: A New English Version* (New York: Free Press, 2006)

> Discover the world's oldest book, originally inscribed on stone tablets in the Akkadian language. This new translation uses modern English to bring the story of Gilgamesh alive. This is a tale of giants and monsters and gods. It is also about friendship and learning to understand one's true nature.

Nardo, Don, *The Greenhaven Encyclopedia of Ancient Mesopotamia* (San Diego: Lucent Books, 2006)

> This well-researched volume gives an overview of the first cities and the cultures of the Sumerians, Assyrians, and Babylonians. The book also looks at the Persian Empire under Cyrus II and Darius I and the invasion by Alexander the Great. Maps and photos add to the text, which is supported by many quotes from primary source documents.

Panchyk, Richard, *Archaeology for Kids: Uncovering the Mysteries of Our Past, 25 Activities* (Chicago: Chicago Review Press, 2001)

> Most of what is known about Mesopotamia and its people has been learned from archaeologists. This book explains what archaeologists do, how they plan their digs, uncover artifacts, and date the items they find. It includes 25 hands-on activities to keep budding archaeologists busy.

Rizza, Alfredo, *The Assyrians and The Babylonians: History and Treasures of an Ancient Civilization* (Boston: White Star Publishers, 2007)

> This well-illustrated book explores the chronology, historic events, key public figures, and cultural legacy of the Assyrian and Babylonian civilizations. The text describes the role played by each group in trade, diplomatic relations, cultural heritage, and military action. Color

photographs show the geography, archaeology, and antiquities of these ancient civilizations, including stone reliefs discovered in royal palaces depicting battle scenes, kings with different gods conducting religious ceremonies, ziggurats, fancy gates guarding the cities, and much more.

Roaf, Michael, *The Cultural Atlas of Mesopotamia and the Ancient Near East* (New York: Facts On File, 1990)

This is a well-researched, well-illustrated study of the geography, history, archaeology, and culture of Mesopotamia and the Near East. It is divided into sections on villages, cities, and empires. Special topics and archaeological sites are featured, described, and illustrated. Some of the topics include the origin of writing, ivory carving, and Mesopotamian warfare. Jericho, Babylon, and Ur are among many archaeological sites that are explained in detail.

DVD

The Kings: From Babylon to Baghdad (The History Channel, 2004)

This DVD tells the story of Iraq through the history of its rulers, from Sargon the Great to Saddam Hussein. Using dialogue drawn directly from original texts of ancient records, *The Kings* depicts ancient events using reenactments. There are also interviews with experts on the historical and current relevance of the area that is today's Iraq.

WEB SITES

Ancient Mesopotamia: This History, Our History
mesopotamia.lib.uchicago.edu/

Learn all about Mesopotamia and the way this culture influences our lives today. This is a virtual museum tour of the Oriental Museum at the University of Chicago. Go on an archaeological dig at a Mesopotamian site. View artifacts that teachers chose specifically to help illustrate Mesopotamian culture. The site offers specific information about daily life, early farming, the invention of writing, religion, the first cities, and a segment about mathematics and methods of measurement.

Ancient West Asia
www.historyforkids.org/learn/westasia/index.htm

All the peoples of ancient West Asia are discussed on this site, including the Persians, Assyrians, Mesopotamians, Babylonians, and others. Each section includes a basic history. A timeline and sections on art, culture, language, religion, clothing, science, and more cover the entire region.

Babylonia, A History of Ancient Babylon
history-world.org/babylonia.htm

This site provides information about Hammurabi and a full explanation of the Code of Hammurabi, which set up the laws of Babylonia. It also tells about the last kings of the empire and the problems they faced ruling Babylonia.

Gateways to Babylon
www.gatewaystobabylon.com

This site about ancient Mesopotamia contains an historical overview, information on religion, myths, magic and the gods, translations of clay tablets, and several classic texts, including the *Epic of Erra and Ishum.*

The Hanging Gardens of Babylon
www.unmuseum.org/hangg.htm

This Web page describes the hanging gardens of Babylon in detail, including a section on how water was carried to them. The other Seven Wonders of the Ancient World are also available for exploration.

The History of Ancient Sumeria
history-world.org/sumeria.htm

From cities and kings to pottery and cuneiform, this site offers a comprehensive view of the Sumerian culture. Click on any of the topics and find a wealth of information. Download examples of cuneiform or review a dictionary of words. Read the Sumerian flood story and compare it to flood legends in history. Investigate the Sumerian calendar, clothing, cities, houses, gods, and the kingdom of Kish.

Internet Ancient History Source Book

www.fordham.edu/halsall/ancient/asbook03. html#Sumeria

This site provides primary source documents from ancient Mesopotamia, including the Code of Hammurabi and the Legend of Gilgamesh. It is ideal for readers looking for primary source materials and information. The site offers links to maps, poems, prayers, epic legends, and information on Sumerian mythology.

Mesopotamia at the British Museum

www.mesopotamia.co.uk

Take a tour through the British Museum's Mesopotamia exhibit. Learn about the geography of the region and see statues and carvings of ancient artworks. The museum provides information about gods, goddesses, and ancient demons. The online exhibit is divided into Assyria, Babylonia, and Sumer. Each section offers interesting information on topics such as the astronomers of Babylon, the palaces of Assyria, and the Sumerian royal tombs of Ur.

Mesopotamian Timeline

www.wsu.edu/~dee/MESO/TIMELINE.HTM

This site from Washington State University offers an extensive timeline of Mesopotamia, including Sumer, Assyria, and Babylon. This is particularly helpful when figuring out which empire was in power during what time period. Click on the timeline for Sumer to learn about Uruk, Ur, and the culture of the Sumerians. The Babylonian timeline offers information about the Akkadians, Amorites, Kassites, and Chaldeans. Read on to find out the history of the Assyrians and the Persians.

PICTURE CREDITS

INDEX

Note: **Boldface** page numbers indicate major discussions of topics; *italic* page numbers indicate illustrations; page numbers followed by *c* indicate chronology entries; page numbers followed by *g* indicate glossary entries; page numbers followed by *m* indicate maps.

witchcraft 41, 104. *See also* magic
women
    Assyrian **112–116**
    Babylonian **90–91**
    business and industry 90
    as chefs 69
    death and burial 106, 109
    depictions of 71, *90, 115*
    harems 115–116
    Kurdish 130
    as priestesses 31, 32, 71, 76, 90, 116
    as queens 76, 82, 115–116
    rights of 71
    as scribes 90
    stoning of 114
    Sumerian **70–71**
    temple work and 76
    as witnesses 71
Woolley, Charles Leonard 37, 82
World War I 126–127
writing. *See* language and writing

Y
yarn 103

Z
Zarima 74
Zarpanit 48, 49
ziggurats 26, *34*, 130, 131, 136g
    Akkadian 33
    pyramids and 26
    Tower of Babel 86
Zimri-Lim 38–39
Ziusudra 79
zodiac 108
zoos 50
Zurma 74

ABOUT THE AUTHOR

BARBARA A. SOMERVILL has written more than 30 books, including biographies of Carrie Chapman Catt, Ida Tarbell, Franklin Pierce, and Mary McLeod Bethune, as well as a history of Korea for young adults. She has also written *Empire of the Incas* and *Empire of the Aztecs* in the Great Empires of the Past series, *Amistad: Fighting for Freedom,* and *Brown v. the Board of Education.*

Historical consultant **LESLIE SCHRAMER** received her Masters Degree in Mesopotamian Archaeology from the University of Chicago in 2003. She has been editor of Serial Publications in the Publications Office at the Oriental Institute of the University of Chicago since 2005. The Oriental Institute is a world-renowned publisher of books on the Near East, from Libya to Iran.